SOCIAL CAPITAL, MIGRATION, ETHNIC DIVERSITY AND ECONOMIC PERFORMANCE

INTERDISCIPLINARY STUDIES ON CENTRAL AND EASTERN EUROPE

Vol. 20

Edited by
Christian Giordano, Nicolas Hayoz & Jens Herlth

PETER LANG

Bern · Bruxelles · Frankfurt am Main · New York · Oxford · Warszawa · Wien

ADNAN EFENDIC, BOJANA BABIC &
ANNA REBMANN

SOCIAL CAPITAL, MIGRATION, ETHNIC DIVERSITY AND ECONOMIC PERFORMANCE

Multidisciplinary Evidence from South-East Europe

PETER LANG

Bern · Bruxelles · Frankfurt am Main · New York · Oxford · Warszawa · Wien

Bibliographic information published by die Deutsche Nationalbibliothek
Die Deutsche Nationalbibliothek lists this publication in the Deutsche National-
bibliografie; detailed bibliographic data is available on the Internet
at ‹http://dnb.d-nb.de›.

British Library Cataloguing-in-Publication Data: A catalogue record for this book
is available from The British Library, Great Britain

Library of Congress Control Number: 2017948458

This study/publication has been produced within the Social Capital and Migration –
Evidence from a Post-Conflict Environment project, which is funded by the Regional
Research Promotion Programme (RRPP). This programme is fully funded by the Swiss
Agency for Development and Cooperation (SDC), Federal Department of Foreign Affairs.

CISAR
Center for Intradisciplinary
social applied research

Regional Research
Promotion Programme | Western Balkans

Cover illustration: Addis A.E.F.

ISBN 978-3-0343-2772-5 hb.   ISBN 978-3-0343-2773-2 eBook
ISBN 978-3-0343-2775-6 MOBI   ISBN 978-3-0343-2774-9 EPUB
ISSN 1661-1349 hb.   ISSN 2235-7025 eBook

This publication has been peer reviewed.

© Peter Lang AG, International Academic Publishers, Bern 2017
Wabernstrasse 40, CH-3007 Bern
bern@peterlang.com, www.peterlang.com

Contents

List of Figures

List of Tables

Acknowledgments

We would like to acknowledge support given to this research by the Regional Research Promotion Programme in the Western Balkans (RRPP), run by the University of Fribourg on a mandate from the Swiss Agency for Development and Cooperation (SDC), Federal Department of Foreign Affairs. We thank the RRPP for financing the project, for training and for various regional and international networking opportunities that we developed through the project. We also acknowledge support from the Center for Intradisciplinary Social Applied Research (CISAR), Sarajevo.

Individuals who supported this project included the RRPP director Nicolas Hayoz, RRPP programme manager Jasmina Opardija-Susnjar, RRPP programme advisor Magdalena Solska and our RRPP local coordinator Dzenana Hrlovic. We would like to thank Aston Business School and, in particular, Professor Tomasz Mickiewicz and Dr Anna Rebmann for their support, as well as our colleagues Dr Hariz Halilovich, Mr Mirza Mujaric, Aleksandra Djordjevic and Aldin Glamocic, who provided important assistance throughout the project. Any weaknesses in this book are the responsibility of the authors.

Adnan Efendic, Bojana Babic and Anna Rebmann

Introduction to Social Capital Specifics of the SEE Region

This book brings together research that focuses on social capital (SC), migration, ethnic diversity and economic performance in the south-east European (SEE) region (Bosnia and Herzegovina, Croatia and Serbia). These affect the social structures of these societies, which are still struggling to rebuild social ties, to control migration and to improve their economic performance, all of which were heavily affected during the 1990s conflict period. These issues are very important for the reintegration of the SEE region more than two decades after the conflicts and for its aspirations towards the EU membership (Croatia already being a member).

These themes are attractive for researchers and have been widely studied in different social science disciplines, including sociology, anthropology and economics – but mainly as separate concepts. This book provides a more comprehensive research effort based on multidisciplinary evidence. We treat these phenomena – social capital, migration, ethnic diversity and economic performance – as interrelated and endogenous and look at them from different angles, investigating them with different research methodologies.

The book does not study relationships between all of these research areas simultaneously but provides a gradual and sequential approach. First, it investigates determinants of social capital in the periods of normality and crisis (floods) that occurred in the region; then it looks how different dimensions of social capital interact with (non)migration experience and later extends this focus to the role of ethnic diversity in affecting social capital of different migrant categories. We end by investigating how ethnic diversity affects the economic performance of individuals and households.

South-eastern Europe – and in particular Bosnia and Herzegovina (BiH) – is a region with one of the most volatile ethnic structures in Europe. Ethnic identities played a crucial role in the 1990s conflicts. To (re)build multiethnic societies it is crucial to understand if ethnicity and ethnic diversity in changed heterogeneous and/or homogeneous ethnic environments influence social capital and the economic performance of individuals and families living in these societies. The outcomes of this research will therefore help to bring about an understanding of the specific situation in the SEE region but also in similar environments elsewhere.

This multidisciplinary and multifocused research uses ideas from different disciplines and theoretical approaches; however, its main contribution to knowledge and policy comes from empirical work based on new data specifically gathered from this part of the SEE region. The book investigates these data using relevant qualitative and quantitative research methodologies with different areas of focus, which examine different dimensions, different relationships and roles of social capital, migration, ethnic diversity and economic performance. Thus, through our research framework, we ask what determines prosocial activities (social capital outcomes) of different people (migrants and nonmigrants) and in different periods (crisis and normality), focusing on relational and structural social capital (inputs). We also investigate how structural dimensions of social capital, considered through ethnic diversity and ethnically diverse networking, affect prosocial engagement, as well as the economic performance of individuals and households.

The quantitative investigations (Chapters 3 and 6) are based on two representative surveys from BiH, implemented in 2015 and 2012. The first (2015) dataset was used to investigate relationships between different dimensions of social capital in normal and crisis periods (periods of natural disaster). It provides an innovative comparative investigation of prosocial behaviour in these different periods. The second (2012) dataset is used to examine the relationships between ethnic diversity and economic performance of individuals and households, which is very relevant to the present time.

The qualitative chapters (Chapters 4 and 5) are based on regional ethnographic research and 100 structured in-depth interviews conducted in the countries of interest. This investigation was implemented with particular reference to different migrant categories (internal and external migrants and internally displaced persons) and, as such, it offers rich qualitative data. This part of the research also provides an innovative approach and is a unique experiment in examining three different migrant categories simultaneously, together with their common and different experiences, their attitudes and their perceptions linked to social capital and ethnic heterogeneity.

Although these empirical sections are interconnected, the chapters also function separately as research essays and readers can select particular areas of research and analysis depending on their interest.

Before presenting the empirical research, the book contains extensive discussion of several theoretical approaches to social capital in the literature (Chapter 2) including Bourdieu (1980), Coleman (1988), Burt (1992) and Putnam (1995). A common feature of these approaches is that the core element of social capital remains relations between people, interactions and approaches to resources, whereas the differences exist mainly in the conceptualization and interpretation of social capital in relation to individuals, networks and social structures.

Our discussion ends with a view of social capital as a multidimensional concept that can be divided into social capital inputs and outputs. Social capital inputs are the vehicles through which social capital can be accumulated (e.g. networks and norms) and social capital outputs (e.g. prosocial behaviour of individuals) are the resources that can be obtained from the social relations (Grooteart *et al.*, 2004). As such, social capital is treated as a positive social phenomenon. This is in line with the majority of the literature, which argues that higher levels of social capital improve political stability, enhance factor productivity and social integration (e.g. Knack and Keefer, 1997; Rose, 1999; Ostrom,1999; Kaasa, 2009; Lesage and Ha, 2012). Moreover, we accept Bierhoff's (2002) argument that social capital is important in producing prosocial behaviour that might be particularly relevant to crisis and postcrisis periods in a society. This argument is empirically tested in the context of our sample. A discussion of the migration and ethnic diversity literature is included in this section. As such, this chapter (Chapter 2) provides a general theoretical introduction to the empirical work that follows rather than a comprehensive theoretical foundation for the whole book. Every following chapter contains its theoretical concepts on which these empirical works rely or make a link to this chapter if necessary to avoid repetition.

The first empirical investigation (Chapter 3) considers prosocial behaviours in crisis periods (the 2014 flood disaster) and normal (postcrisis) periods. We distinguish between social capital outcomes (prosocial behaviour) and social capital inputs, which, together with other determinants of social capital (individual and socioeconomic) explain social capital on the ground, proxied by the prosocial activities of citizens. This research considers these two types of activities in a joint system with a wider list of causalities coming from observed and unobserved endogenous influences. The research suggests that if individuals engage in a greater number of social activities in a period when there is no crisis they display more engagement in a period of crisis. Although this outcome is logical, it indicates that building social capital in normal times or everyday life is an investment for greater security when society is confronted with sudden challenges and crises. Chapter 3 also investigates the effect of individual and household socioeconomic characteristics on prosocial activities in different periods, as well as the effect of formal and informal economic activities on social capital.

One of the important structural networking dimensions covered is the ethnic diversity of networks. This is a particularly relevant determinant for ethnically mixed societies, such as the SEE region. There is a published research that identifies the positive effects of ethnic diversity on growth aspirations and business development in BiH (Efendic *et al.*, 2015). This study also reports a complementary finding for the household sector – personal network (ethnic) diversity is beneficial for prosocial behaviour in both, normal and crisis periods.

Chapter 4 provides a qualitative analysis of the underlying determinants of SC among migrants and nonmigrants in Bosnia and Herzegovina and in the neighbouring countries of Serbia and Croatia. The aim of this section is to investigate core determinants further, including economic, postconflict, ethnic, religious and individual factors that influence the SC of individuals, differentiated by their migration status, in a postconflict environment. The qualitative investigation of the social relationships between people finds that the ongoing economic and political transformation processes in the SEE region are linked to the SC outcomes on the ground. This has resulted in changed and often imposed social norms and social relations. For example, the relational dimension of SC suggests that a lack of general trust in institutions and people is common in all three SEE countries and all social strata examined, although slight differences might exist at local levels. Structural SC largely replaces and compensates for the lack of trust in the postconflict societies. At the same time, structural SC indicates that migrant experiences, ethnicity and resulting feelings of social exclusion, for both migrant and nonmigrant groups are important, but not crucial in their everyday lives. Migrant experiences might influence the relationships at the individual or group/association level in terms of people's exclusion (but also inclusion in certain groups) from the places where they have settled or resettled but the same perceptions are also often identified for nonmigrants. People quite often rely on their migrant experiences for solidarity and empathy, among other things. Various examples of solidarity or empathy might be found among those with different migrant or nonmigrant experiences, particularly at the local levels such as in urban neighbourhoods, or rural and semirural areas, in various organizations/associations and so on. Together with personal socioeconomic characteristics, which are the most important features of SC for all groups examined, the question about how SC is transferred from individual to "community" level and distributed to all actors has yet to be explored.

Social capital has played an important role in the (re)integration processes of the migrant and nonmigrant populations in the postconflict environments of the SEE region. Specifically, based on the collected data, we are able to identify that challenges in the political and economic environments – resulting in a lack of trust in institutions and people – have been replaced by specific trust in certain individuals, institutions and social networks among all three migrant groups in focus. These emerging social relationships and norms therefore require further investigation where they take place. Generally, in (re)building multiethnic societies in postwar environments such as BiH, it is crucial to understand how ethnicity and ethnic diversity in changed heterogeneous and homogeneous ethnic environments influence social capital. Specifically, it is important to explore how ethnicity intersects with other sociocultural characteristics such as gender, age and class and how it operates in relation to the main dimensions of SC: trust, networks and prosocial behaviour. This chapter (Chapter 5) addresses these issues in a systematic manner. The discussion in this chapter is based on four case studies that include both ethnically homogenous and heterogeneous environments and for all three migrant groups in focus, including nonmigrant and across three different SEE countries: Banja Luka (Republika Srpska, BiH), Bugojno (Federation of BiH, BiH), Novi Sad (Serbia) and Plaški (Croatia).

It was a significant challenge to link ethnicity and ethnic diversity with the main dimensions of SC under consideration, although this chapter is based on a rich qualitative material collected in SEE region. However, the results imply that different political and economic environments, along with individual socioeconomic characteristics and migrant status, do influence SC in both ethnically homogenous and heterogeneous environments. In addition, the minority and majority relationships between and within three ethnic groups in the homogenous and heterogeneous ethnic communities and societies are experienced differently on the ground.

The last empirical chapter (Chapter 6) investigates whether ethnic diversity is associated with individual and household economic performance. In our analysis, we focus on BiH, a postconflict transition country, which is a particularly appropriate context for such a study. Throughout its thousand-year-long history, BiH had been recognized as a multicultural environment, mixing, accommodating and adopting different Eastern and Western cultural, religious and political influences. Even today, more than two decades after the brutal 1992–1995 war, BiH remains a multicultural country with one of the most "complicated" ethnic structures in Europe. We would also like to add that this is not only something to be acknowledged and recognized as "complicated" but also a social reality that should be celebrated and promoted. This empirical investigation links the ethnic diversity of neighbouring areas with core microeconomic theory (Mincer, 1974) and investigates whether ethnic diversity is associated with individual and household income. As such, this research represents a pioneering multidisciplinary approach that brings a policy message to the research community but, equally importantly, to the policymakers of this region. Our result implies that ethnic heterogeneity is not a threat to the economic prosperity of individuals and households but, rather, that it is a benefit that improves their economic performance.

Bojana Babic, Adnan Efendic and Anna Rebmann

Social Capital, Migration, Ethnic Diversity and Economic Performance in the Literature

Introduction

In this chapter we present a brief introduction and overview of the theoretical and empirical literature on social capital, migration, ethnic diversity and economic performance. Understanding the concept of social capital in a multidisciplinary context is a research challenge that is introduced in the first section, which provides an explanation of the approach to social capital used in this study. The conceptual differences in definitions of social capital create considerable difficulty with regard to adequate measurement of, or proxying for, social capital – in particular because different dimensions of social capital can be treated as inputs (independent variables) and/ or outputs (dependent variables). This chapter will discuss approaches to measuring social capital in the literature, and will conclude that a common measure of social capital does not exist.

There is a lot of heterogeneity in the literature, reflecting diverse theoretical approaches to the issue of social capital, migration, ethnic diversity and economic performance. However, there are also practical solutions in gathering missing data on social capital and some promising ideas that can be applied in the context of our investigation. Indeed, a targeted survey seems to be the most widely used approach and the one that can tell the most about this social phenomenon. This strategy is used in this book.

The next section identifies what determines social capital performance and its changes and what the potential consequences are for other socioeconomic outputs. Thus, the book includes a discussion of the main determinants of social capital, recognizing potential factors that need to be linked to the region in focus and the empirical investigation that follows. We aim to link social capital to different migrant categories of population living in these postconflict societies, so one section also offers a discussion on potential links between social capital and migration. Finally, ethnic diversity, as the concept that is used in majority of empirical chapters in the study, is also introduced with an emphasis on how ethnic diversity might be linked to social capital and economic performance at different levels of analysis. This chapter therefore serves the purpose of acquainting the reader with the basic terms, concepts, relationships and existing empirical findings relevant to the research that follows. However, for those who are more familiar with the literature, reading the empirical chapters might be enough, as they are organized as independent contributions to the book and all of them contain their specific links to the relevant literature.

Understanding the Concept of Social Capital

The concept of social capital has gained a lot of attention in the academic and policymaking world, especially recently. Kwon and Adler (2014) even argue that social capital – generally defined as the goodwill available to individuals and groups – has already matured from a concept into a whole field of research. Some scholars refer to it as a heuristic device (Christoforou and Davis, 2014) or an ambiguous concept (Hellermann, 2006), whereas some are rather critical of the whole social capital idea (Portes, 1998). Nevertheless, it is hard to ignore the fact that social capital has become a growth industry (Baker and Faulkner, 2009) and that the research focus on social capital has multiplied rapidly over the last two decades in particular (Kwon and Adler, 2014).

The term "capital" is used to emphasize that, along with financial, physical, human and cultural capital, "societal" aspects of individuals and groups can be important for economic outcomes as well. It is "capital" because it can be transferred into other forms of economic capital (Righi, 2013). Financial, physical and human capitals are not used in isolation but require interactions between people (Woolcock, 1998). As a consequence, the content and structure of relationships can have a large impact on individual, societal, economic and overall situations. For example, the stock of social capital might be related to issues such as (political) institutional efficiency, economic development, crime rates and reduced incidences of other social and environmental problems (Lesage and Ha, 2012). Higher levels of social capital may improve political stability, factor productivity and entrepreneurship, provision of public goods, economic growth and social integration (e.g. Knack and Keefer, 1997; Ostrom, 1999; Rose, 1999; Kaasa, 2009; Lesage and Ha, 2012). Social capital, as such, can serve as a link between social cooperation, progressive politics and forward-looking economics (Pieterse, 2003), but we need to understand its *theoretical, policy and measurement* frameworks and the links between them (Edwards *et al.*, 2006).

The *theoretical basis of the concept of social capital* today results from a mixture of three main theoretical traditions: critical, rational and functionalist, developed by the French sociologist Pierre Bourdieu (1980), James Coleman (1993a, 1993b) and Robert Putnam (1993, 1995). A number of other scholars contributed to the concepts, such as Loury (1977), Burt (1992) and others. However, Bourdieu's, Coleman's and Putnam's theories remain the core focus of researchers. Each theory's concepts are elaborated briefly below.

Pierre Bourdieu held a more critical perspective and understood social capital as potentially the reproduction of inequality (Grossman, 2013). He defined social capital as "the aggregate of the actual potential resources that are linked to possession of a durable network of more of less institutionalized relationships of mutual acquaintance or recognition" (Bourdieu, 1986, p. 248). For Bourdieu, social capital is indistinguishable from economic, cultural and symbolic capital. The investment of material resources and the possession of some cultural knowledge enable individuals to establish their relations with others (Portes, 2000), which might be used to upgrade their place in the hierarchy. Bourdieu's focus was on the social hierarchy embedded in society and how people use different tactics to be successful in the hierarchies based on the differential distribution of the four specific capitals (Grossman, 2013). Bourdieu's operationalization of the four forms of social capital is framed in the context of social space, fields and practice. According to him, social practice, understood as a link between body and practice within the social world, creates its own rules, scheme of domination, legitimate opinions, and so forth, which leads to the establishment of a social field. Social fields became spaces in which people relate and struggle through a complexity of connected social relations and where the social practice may therefore appear as "the permanent internalisation of the social order in the human body" (Bourdieu, 1986). It is actually through social practice that the relative reproduction and distribution of resources and their activation are possible (Tzanakis, 2013). As a consequence a certain kind of gain (financial or nonfinancial), social capital might lead to both inequality and social justice within the society. It depends on actors, who are unequal in possessing and activating their resources, together with the size of the network and the volume of past accumulated social capital. The potentially exclusionary side of social capital (Gauntlet, 2011) and possibilities of social capital being used to produce and reproduce inequality, which supports social stratification (Bourdieu, 1983), remain an important consideration.

Bourdieu's understanding of social capital has been relevant to the issues of increasing social marginalization and the emergence of different forms of inequality. This has been criticized, however. The main critique refers to its lack of alternatives and its reductionism in privileging economic capital as the ultimate source of all other capital, which are eventually exchanged for it (Alexander, 1976; Jenkins, 1992). Bourdieu regards social capital exclusively as class based. In this way he limits the meaning of social, economic, cultural and symbolic social capital, which then become context specific and cannot be seen within a broader framework of social life.

In comparison to Bourdieu, James Coleman's more rational orientation is related to his notion that social capital resides in social structures of relationships between actors and among actors. He defines social capital within certain aspects of social structure which facilitates certain actions of actors – whether persons or corporate actors – within the border social environment (Coleman, 1988, p. 90). Social capital gathers goal-oriented actors who use it as a collective resource to achieve particular goals. For Coleman, social capital resides in the ties between people, such as networks, and it is not privately held (Coleman, 1988). He further acknowledges that having relationships with others is a social form of "capital" because ties contain resources. For him social capital is a resource in itself (Grossman, 2013). To that end, a property shared by most forms of social capital that differentiates it from other forms of capital is the fact that it is a public good (Coleman, 1988). At the same time, he emphasizes the importance of family-based social capital but also indicates that social capital is not necessarily owned and it might arise as an available resource (Gauntlet, 2011). To gain access to social capital a person usually needs to invest some time and effort in building and gaining trust. The actor's actions are therefore shaped, redirected and constrained by social context, norms and interpersonal trust, social networks and social organizations (Coleman, 1988).

For Coleman there are three forms of social capital: (i) obligations and expectations, which depend on the trustworthiness of social environment, (ii) the ability of the social structure to support the flow of information and (iii) social norms accompanied by sanctions. For Coleman, trust is essential for all three forms of social capital. Trust in a social structure or society as well as social norms reflects the existence of social capital itself. Furthermore, for Coleman, social capital provides the possibility of combining different resources in order to produce different system-level behaviour and values within social organisations. The value of the concept of social capital lies in the fact that it identifies certain aspects of social structure by their function, which actors might use as a resource to achieve certain ends. This function of certain aspects of social structure might enable different outcomes for individual actors and social organizations (micro-to-macro transition). To achieve certain benefits community ties should engage individuals with various personal characteristics (Portes, 2000). The social capital might then become an attribute of the community itself, including even the powerless and marginalized (Gauntlet, 2011) – and a potential resource along with human, physical or economic capital. Although these effects of social capital should be mainly positive, problems actually exist in micro-to-macro transition, a transition from individual to community level, within certain social structures.

However, Coleman's understanding of social capital has received various criticisms. First, there is a difficulty in distinguishing between resources and the ability of network members to obtain them (Portes, 1998; Quibria, 2003). Second, the frequently generalization of a positive community-level output of social capital for all people might cause the concept of social capital to became vague and abstract, which limits its further use (Lin, 1999; Portes, 2000; Quibria, 2003). Third, the closure of social capital without a possibility of access to the others outside the network limits an understanding of social capital in the broader social context (Burt, 1992; Lin, 1999; Fukuyama, 2001). Fourth, social capital is context dependent and therefore context specific in regard to resources, attitudes and norms such as trust and reciprocity or social network accumulations (Edwards, 1999; Shucksmith, 2000). There is a lack of attention to structural inequalities and power relations (Fraser and Lacey, 1993; Molyneux, 2002; Tonkiss, 2000; Edwards *et al.*, 2003). Finally, a feminist critiques of possible gender-power relationships emerging within families (Molyneux, 2002).

Finally, Robert Putnam's interest in social capital is in volunteering and civic action as well as democracy and community (Grossman, 2013). He locates social capital in social ties between actors or within a community's network of relations (Putnam, 2000). Putnam's interpretation of social capital refers to the broader societal context and the importance of the collective value of all social actions that arise from these networks for building up democracy, civic engagement and communal health (Putnam, 2000). Putnam defined social capital as "feature of social organizations, such as networks, norms and trust that facilitate actions and cooperation for mutual benefit" (Putnam, 1993, p. 35). For him, social capital is a quality that can facilitate interpersonal cooperation, even at the level of cities, regions and countries. To build social capital, a certain level of trust is required and it should be achieved within civil society. Trust and civic engagement provide citizens with norms of strong associational participation and cooperation on economic and political projects. Accordingly, social capital facilitates the formal co-ordination mechanisms in modern economies by reducing transaction costs (Fukuyama, 2001) and prizing informal, voluntary networks in democratic societies. Trust therefore remains in the core of his conceptualization of social capital because of its link to the norm of reciprocity as well as the broad and localized benefits that are derived from social or generalized trust (Putnam, 1993, 2001). His notion of "thin" (trust embedded in personal relationships that are strong, frequent, and nested in wider networks) and "thick" (extends trust beyond an individual's actual network, and it is based more on community norms than personal experience, therefore if the community connections deteriorate) trust views them as important features of the network, providing the structure necessary for social capital. Within this framework, Putnam explains a possibility of social capital to be achieved and practised through "bridging" and "bonding" (Putnam, 2001). *Bridging* should increase cohesion between different groups and *bonding* should expand the networks within a given group. Together they bring positive results for a society. Ties achieved through bridging and bounding remain central for analysis in regard to a positive association between social capital and outputs such as civic engagement, economic prosperity and the growth of (democratic) citizenship. Stronger ties within a given group are not always desirable for the network between the groups. As Savioli and Patuelli (2016) pointed out, weaker ties between the networks create larger networks and better sharing of information.

Putnam's formulation of social capital has been subjected to various criticisms. The main critiques of Putnam's formulation of social capital concern his treatment of trust and the ways in which it is linked – not equally distributed in a network or equally accessible by all actors (Tzanakis, 2013). His interpretation equates the sources of social capital with its outcomes but fails to deliver the conditions under which social networks represent effects of social capital and whether social capital is a consequence or determinant (Portes, 1998, 2000; Morrow, 1999; Narayan and Cassidy, 2001; Sobel, 2002; Adam and Roncevic, 2003). A further criticism is that he assumes that a high level of social capital already exists (Portes, 1998, Brucker, 1999; Foley and Edwards, 1999). He isolates a single factor as an explanation for the growth of the economy and democracy (Portes, 1998; Edwards, 1999). He analyses trust at a regional and country level without looking at the individual level. In other words, he fails to question the context of social capital and understands it as something that emerges between individuals rather than solely to the level of the region or the country as a commonly shared quality (Foley and Edwards, 1999; Stryker and Burke, 2000; Smith and Kulynych, 2002; Edwards *et al.*, 2003). He frequently neglects differences in networks, both horizontally (with regard to the type and value of resources, and the type of ties available at a certain point of time) and vertically (with regard to the location of actors and the level of aggregation) (Foley and Edwards, 1999; Kearns and Parkinson, 2001). He insists on the temporal dimension in network operation and fails to conceptualize whether a certain norm that has emerged through social capital, such as trust, will be available to a person all the time (Adam and Roncevic, 2003; Sobel, 2002; Morrow, 1999). Finally there is a failure to account adequately for human agency because the actors who occupy different locations might be different persons and may react differently to the context in the same network (Tzanakis, 2013).

Common to Bourdieu's, Coleman's and Putnam's theoretical approaches to social capital is the idea that the concept relates to people, interactions, networks and resources (Bourdieu, 1977, 1980; Coleman, 1988; Putnam, 1993, 2000). The main distinction is in their conceptualization and interpretation regarding the relations of the individuals, networks and social structures. Both Coleman and Bourdieu focus on the context of the structure of relationships and issues of power, although with different perspectives.

Bourdieu reflects the Marxist concern about unequal access to resources and unequal access to power. For Coleman the starting points are the rational actions of individuals to pursue their own interests in linking structure and agency. Putnam refers to social integration and wellbeing through ideas of association and civic activity (Field, 2003). Furthermore, while Coleman and Putnam focus on the actors within structure of networks and content of the relations, Bourdieu brings theory inequality and social justice into his theory (Edwards *et al.*, 2006). Putnam contextualizes social capital through bridging and bounding, whereas Coleman goes for obligations and expectations, norms and information channels. For both, the core of social capital is in trust. Bourdieu, however, is not explicitly focused on trust. Furthermore, for Bourdieu and Coleman, the centre of social capital studies is small groups or individuals, while Putnam focuses on community, cities, regions and even nations. Coleman and Putnam see the potential of social capital as an advantage of democratic and market-oriented societies, whereas, for Bourdieu, social orders that have emerged through social capital might even support and maintain inequalities. Overall, Coleman and Putnam are more explicit in regarding social capital as isolated from other forms of capital than Bourdieu (Grossman, 2013). At the same time, Coleman and Putnam's concepts have been perceived as easier to operationalize and put in practice for policymaking than Bourdieu's.

Due to the difficulty in understanding people's social lives and social relationships, many agree that social capital presents a complex concept that needs to be properly defined and applied in both research and policymaking (Onyx and Bullen, 2000; Lesage and Ha, 2012). These complexities are a consequence of a number of controversies linked to the concept of social capital itself such as its application to different types of social issues, to its use in theories involving different units of analysis, to the fact that it is poorly defined and less tangible than physical and human capital and to its limited effect outside the group (Onyx and Bullen, 2000; Portes, 2000; Goulbourne and Solomos, 2003; Lesage and Ha, 2012). Moreover, very often a concept of social capital is applied as universal for all groups at all times, without taking into consideration its fluidity and shifts over the time (Coleman, 1988; Putnam, 2000). In contrast, a number of scholars suggest that different groups living in different contexts and with various experiences might experience social capital differently (Grossman, 2013). The common feature for many is the difficulty in transferring it from an individual level to an aggregated level (Tzanakis, 2013). There is also a danger that social capital could become a "catch-all" concept (Grossman, 2013; Field, 2003), which would influence its policy relevance and make it difficult to measure.

The conceptualization of social capital in terms of resources and the distinction between having and using social capital (Kwon and Adler, 2014) remain important features for the operationalization of the concept. It is seen as a social resource that emerges through the relationship between individuals, groups and networks, which can be accessed and used to reach individual or collective goals (Bourdieu, 1980; Coleman, 1988; Putnam, 1993, 2000; Lin, 1999). This means that a variety of social capital dimensions might be addressed and measured. The dimensions of social capital have been used to interpret its multifaceted functions in economics and societies (Savioli and Patuelli, 2016). Moreover, the dimensions might cover different aspects at both the structural and individual level such as social skills, trust, reciprocity, exchange, obligation, in-groups, norms, values systems, ethnicity and religious, identity (Bourdieu, 1980, 1986; Coleman, 1988; Nahapiet and Ghoshal, 1998; Portes, 1998; Lin, 1999; Putnam, 2001; Alder and Know, 2002; Grossman, 2013).

Savioli and Patuelli (2016) have divided these dimensions into structural, relational and cognitive. The structural domain, which refers to the structural environment with its roles, rules, precedence and procedures (Uphoff, 2000), is particularly important for understanding the relational aspects of social life, such as organizational, institutional and leadership aspects, at the group level. The relational aspect of social capital therefore pertains to trust, norms and identity (Savioli and Patuelli, 2016). In most cases trust represents a fundamental dimension of social capital that can have both positive and negative effects, depending mainly on whether it produces positive externalities or competence or control (Nooteboom, 2007). The cognitive domain refers to mental processes, concepts and ideas articulated through value systems, ethnic, religious and other principles embedded in language, stories and culture (Savioli and Patuelli, 2016). It is important to understand how social groups communicate and share these mental processes, whether it produces a certain level of trust, and if so, how and for whom. It is also important to acknowledge whether individuals might take advantage of their network, how and why.

Critiques of social capital very often raise the question of the relationship between policy implementation and social capital. Does the concept, with its focus on particular aspects of social life together with a trust in its influence on policymakers, hide more than it illuminates or is it even harmful (Edwards *et al.*, 2006)? In order to influence everyday practices in relation to building social integration, social capital became a tool for various policymaking actions. These actions vary from the impulse to control contemporary liberal societies, which are increasingly diverse and undergo rapid social change. A desire to reintroduce a normative dimension of how society works and includes a concern with the excesses of current individualism and nostalgia for a lost cohesive past is frequently missed (Edwards *et al.*, 2009). Long-lasting relationships represented through networks are based on trust and reciprocity (Savioli and Patuelli, 2016). By and large their strength depends on ties built up through time, emotional involvement and intimacy. Consequently, many of these factors might further reinforce a normative perception assigned to particular networks and their actions while excluding those who are frequently already on the margins. Status therefore remains an important factor in social capital.

Nevertheless, driven mostly by Coleman's rational action model and Putman's link between social capital and economic development, the concept of social capital is welcomed among policymakers. Numerous governments such as the US, Australian, Canadian and UK governments and many others have encouraged different policies based on social capital assumptions. Moreover, in the context of current crises, the concept of social capital brings possible solutions in bridging the gap between market and state, in implementing liberal free-market policies and welfare systems and finally in the inclusion of social considerations in the economic sphere (Edwards *et al.*, 2006). At the same time the policies of social capital showed various constraints, lacking an understanding of the complexity of the condition of the social sphere, or the functions and effects of social action and the overall situation on the ground. Moreover, to a certain extent there is no guarantee that that public policies that embrace social capital might work in the best interest of society. Policymakers frequently fail to consider that social capital is still very much linked to the family connections and has a time dimension. The behaviour of people frequently depends on their particular situation, which might change over time. Social segmentation might be reinforced by different elements such as various income and ethnicity factors or mobility of population (Alesina and La Ferrara, 2002). Therefore, actions of policymakers tend to be focused more on a kind of capital. Instead of accessing policies through the physical capital an initiative could address human capital to improve people's wellbeing.

This brings us to the possibility of *measuring the concept of social capital*, understood as practice and modelling. The main aim is to show what constitutes social capital and how social networks and collective actions, common norms and expectations, rewards in the form of resources and sanctions that restrict access to them, trust and reciprocity, function on the ground. At the same time, to identify causal relationships behind the important outcomes of social capital through cross-sectional and longitudinal investigation, more experimental designs are needed (Tzanakis, 2013). Furthermore, social capital should be expanded to include nonlinear or circular forms (Smith and Kulnych, 2002). The context and time dimension should be taken into account more seriously.

In order to achieve this goal, several as yet unexplored areas should be taken into account. An important gap in social capital practice and modelling is a lack of common theoretical frameworks to explain intergroup and between-group relationships. Intergroup conflicts (Goette *et al.*, 2006) and conflict resolution (Poletta and Jasper, 2001) require interdisciplinary attention (Tzanakis, 2013). This potentially requires more attention to the social theories of identity and inequality. For example, group (ethnic) identity might both limit and facilitate access to resources and therefore affect and be affected by social capital. That again depends on the concept of social capital and group identity. In the same manner, social capital is ambivalent in the context of inequality; it could be both a cause and a consequence of social inequality (Tzanakis, 2013). This has been addressed, in particular, by organizational studies that showed various examples of the importance of social capital for inter- and intraorganizational co-ethnic organizations (Light, 2001). Again, the overall results would depend on assumptions regarding the meaning of public good, the dynamics of ethnic families and social space.

Given this background and the need for our research to investigate determinants of social capital in a postconflict environment (BiH, Serbia and Croatia), we situated our theoretical framework on several concepts adopted by all three prominent theories. More precisely, we aimed to combine different approaches to understanding and measuring social capital following Grootaert *et al.*'s (2003) methodology, which assumes a multi-level and multidimensional integrated concept of social capital.

Accordingly, we understand social capital as a multidimensional phenomenon, which includes groups and networks, trust and solidarity, collective action and prosocial behaviour. We adopt this multidimensional approach in measuring social capital in a postconflict environment.

Measuring Social Capital

Measuring or proxying social capital is a challenging task for several reasons. First, the different theoretical approaches explained earlier have consequences for social capital measurement (Righi, 2013). Second, many agree today that social capital is a multidimensional concept that is, by definition, not easy to measure (Grootaert *et al.*, 2004; Diez, 2013). Third, dealing with social capital multidimensionality, researchers have already considered different levels of social capital analysis in practice (macro-meso-micro). The macroconcept of social capital focuses on societal relations (widely shared social norms as trust and reciprocity), while the microcontext focus on personal relations (size and properties of social networks). Fourth, it is a capital that is less visible than standard factors of production – physical and human capital (Lesage and Ha, 2012).

In order to capture more dimensions of social capital in their measurements, some authors rely on composite and aggregated indices of social capital (Grootaert *et al.*, 2004; Aleksander, 2007). Cristoforou (2011) established an index of civic participation as a composite index of membership in a list of association and used it as a proxy for social capital. This measure of social capital is regressed on a set of individual and aggregated determinants of social capital. Alexander (2007) relies on an aggregated index of social capital, which includes a number of determinants such as: club meetings attended last year, community projects worked on last year, times entertained at home last year, time volunteered last year and some other variables from social-capital-related questions focused on generalized trust, honesty and time spent visiting friends. They also include some indicators such as a state's registered nonprofit organizations per capita and the percentage of people serving on a local organization committee. As can be seen, this index of social capital integrates a number of determinants from different levels of analysis. Alexander's index of social capital includes determinants related to a timing effect of socialization, which in Garcia Diez's (2013) explanation is also a good strategy to measure social capital. The author argues that studying the time dedicated to others or spent by individuals and households on providing goods and services outside the market is the measure and concept that should be welcomed.

A multidimensional and a multilevel approach to measuring social capital is recommended by Grootaert *et al.* (2004), who present an integrated questionnaire, which should help and guide researchers in measuring social capital and generating quantitative data. These authors recognize six dimensions of social capital, including groups and networks, trust and solidarity, collective action and cooperation, information and communication, social cohesion and inclusion, empowerment and political action. However, these authors make it clear that every country might have locally important issues as well as different formulations of questions related to understanding these different dimensions of social capital.

The literature identifies several critiques of different measures of social capital. Righi (2013) raised some concerns about measuring social capital. First, while the concept of social capital is generally recognized as multidimensional, much research uses a single dimension or indicator, which is hardly acceptable today. Second, the literature recognizes different levels of social capital, primarily micro-macro determinants, while some research is focused only on individual/micro dimensions, ignoring the macrofoundations of social capital. Thirdly, some studies use outcomes of social capital (e.g. levels of crime) as a proxy for weak social capital, which is also hardly to accept. Finally, conventional surveys usually do not capture more aspects of social capital, which might be improved through targeted surveys.

Although it is possible to identify a good number of strategies and measures used in the literature, which sometimes confuse the reader, these different measures or proxies are often reflections of data availability. A targeted survey that can ensure multidimensional and multilevel measurements of the social capital, including local context, appears to be the most promising approach and the one that we use in this study. Accordingly, our aim is to consider social capital from a multidimensional and multilevel perspective and that should include relevant aspects of social capital recognized in the literature, as well as some related local specifics. This approach not only integrates different dimensions and levels of investigation, but it integrates the main theoretical approaches used to understand social capital. The main discussion of the application of our data to the social capital measurement may be found in Chapter 3.

Determinants of Social Capital

Determinants of social capital are often presented as a set of individual or aggregated factors, which consider social participation as an outcome of investment decision or contextual influence (Christoforou, 2011). Individual factors are frequently interpreted as the social means for personal economic gains, while aggregated factors are related to the processes of socialization and political discourses, which affect social welfare. An important division in the social capital literature is the level of analysis – if social capital is more a macro-level phenomenon (Putnam, 2000) or more a micro-level phenomenon linked to individuals (Bourdieu, 1986). Some even recognize meso-level determination of social capital. For example, in the context of a business environment and the role of social capital in supporting growth aspirations of young companies, Efendic *et al.* (2015) investigated social capital as a multidimensional and multilevel phenomenon focusing on micro-level, meso-level and macro-level determinants. Similarly, Garip (2008) differentiate three dimensions of migration social capital (based on data from rural villages in Thailand), namely individual characteristics, household and village performance.

Earlier work on determinants of social capital mostly investigated the impact of individual and group characteristics on individuals' membership within the structural environment (Glaeser *et al.*, 2002). For example, very often individual characteristics such as personal income and education resulted in higher social capital (Hellermann, 2006); a reason for that has been interpreted as the social status that those people have within societies or it is suggested that they enjoy more social interaction. Pieterse (2003) distinguishes between strong ties (close relations) and weak ties (distant relations) as important determinants of social capital. Other resources of determinants of social capital indicated the importance of age, life experiences, professional qualifications, gender and work as features of social capital accumulation decisions. At the same time, macro characteristics might be modest in comparison to the effects of individual attributes of political orientation, personal freedom, moral sense, religiosity and life satisfaction (Christoforou, 2011). That very much depends on how individual assessments of social obligation reflect norms and values that are shaped and sustained at a more aggregated level (Christoforou, 2011). These arguments should be presented by impacts in the context of determined factors (Costa and Khan, 2003). For example, income inequality, birthplace fragmentation and different social roles of women and men play important roles in individuals' participation in organizations. There are arguments that social capital depends not only on individual experiences but also on characteristics of the community that are influenced by socialization processes and public institutions as well (Brehm and Rahn, 1997).

Here are some examples of empirical work. Mondejar-Jimenez *et al.* (2013) investigated determinants of social capital in Central European countries and focused primarily on individual factors, institutional trust and social and political participation in these countries as determinants of social capital. Alexander (2007) investigated determinants of social capital at the state level, focusing primarily on religion, ethnic diversity and economic determinants (poverty, unemployment, income). The author identifies the strongest determinants of social capital levels as social and economic differences, including education, religion, farming and unemployment. Alexander also identified the link between ethnic diversity and social capital.

Hellermann (2006) identified social capital as being very much linked to economic capital, in particular in the early stages of migration – and it is not only context tied but also gendered. Efendic *et al.* (2015) investigated social capital as a determinant of entrepreneurial growth aspirations of young companies. This study analyses micro-level determinants of social capital (network size and characteristics), meso-level factors (generalized and institutional trust) and macro-level context (ethnic and institutional structure). Social capital determinants linked to all levels of analysis appear to be important in affecting growth aspirations.

To conclude, in order to understand the probability of an individual being a member of a group, social networks and values of reciprocity and cooperation should be investigated through individual determinants such as education, employment, income, sex, age, gender, marital status and other characteristics. At the same time, a number of studies confirm that group membership is strongly affected by aggregated variables. The importance of systems, country-specific factors influenced by history and culture, the welfare system, the political environment, ethnic diversity, labour-market conditions, marriage conventions and roles should not be neglected. Moreover, these two sides should interlink and consolidate the impact of institutional context and its interaction with individual choices (generalized and institutional trust).

Social Capital and Migration

Factors that affect (e)migration often overlap with social capital determinants. They are often presented through different understandings of migration as a process, applied to different types of social issues and used in theories involving different units of analysis. In an early but influential work, Ravenstein (1889) concluded that the most important determinant that affects migration is the desire of most humans to achieve a better material status; simply, it is the economic status of individuals that is the main driver of migration. Many authors still see economic factors as the first determinant of migration (Ravenestein, 1889; Caragliu *et al.*, 2012). Indeed, they see it not just as the first factor but as the factor that often overwhelms the effect of other influences (Constantinou and Diamantides, 1985). Simply, prevailing socioeconomic conditions create a pool of potential migrants and the economic performance of a country is a good predictor of migration (Bahna, 2008).

However, the functionalist model (focusing primarily on economic/ structural determinants) fails to include or explain personal factors and the possibility that individuals can be active actors in migration processes (de Haas, 2011). Instead, society is considered as a system or an aggregate made of interdependent parts with a tendency towards equilibrium (de Haas, 2011). That also includes a possible explanation of migration through the macro-level geographical differences in the supply of and demand for labour, as well as through the micro-level environment where individuals are presented as rational and income-maximizing actors.

These assumptions rarely see people's agency and other determinants such as states, networks and institutions, which might emerge through their personal factors and their ability to make individual choices and potentially structure migration processes. For example, Lee (1966), Haug

(2008) and Brockerhoff and Eu (1993) identify personal factors/features that should be investigated as potential drivers of migration, where age, education, gender and marital status might be determinants influencing migration aspirations. A particularly common research concern is skilled migration, recognized either as the brain-drain effect or, depending on the context, as a brain-gain effect, which has been widely investigated in the literature. From one side, the brain-drain argument is that educated and skilled individuals tend to migrate more than less educated ones (Akee, 2010; Gibson and McKenzie, 2011). The main explanation comes from the human capital theory – higher qualifications increase the probability of finding a job or a better paid job (Haug, 2008). On the other hand, a country's stock of human capital may increase as a consequence of migration. The opportunity to migrate in the future incentivizes potential migrants to invest in their education; hence, this might lead to brain gain in some countries (Stark *et al.*, 1997; Beine *et al.*, 2001; Stark, 2004). Moreover, cultural (Caragliu *et al.*, 2012), political (Constantinou and Diamantides, 1985; Efendic, 2016), demographic (Brockerhoff and Eu, 1993) and ethnic determinants (Docquier and Rapoport, 2004) of migration aspirations have been identified as important in the literature (Zbinden et al., 2016). In the context of ethnicity migration prospects sometimes have a protective effect on the minority (Docquier and Rapoport, 2004), which might be a particularly relevant issue for postethnic conflict environments.

Migration can also be explained as collective household strategies (Stark, 1991, Stark and Bloom, 1985, Taylor, 1999) that tend to overcome market failures and spread income risks. Simply, migration might be a family strategy (Haug, 2008). For example, in order to overcome structural constraints, remittances might be used as a family livelihood strategy to raise investment capital. However, it is important not to neglect important migration determinants such as market access, income inequality, relative deprivation and social security.

In order to overcome this obstacle of different levels and units of analysis it is important to incorporate these various determinants of migration into the broader picture. Interlinks between macrostructural factors such as states, policies, labour markets, status hierarchies, power inequalities and social group formation and individuals might be explained through analysis of the group – family, community, society – and reproduction of patterns as relations between people (de Haas, 2011). Furthermore, a potential gap between macrostructural and meso-group level might be filled by important microcharacteristics such as the effects of age, gender, skill, ethnicity, regional and other factors on collective action. In that respect, the effects of economic transformations might go further than the reproduction and reinforcement of structural inequalities and power relations. From a methodological point of view, authors also appear to adopt a multilevel approach in their analysis of migration, as in the social capital literature. The multilevel analysis includes primarily macroapproaches, based on analytical models and macroeconomic determinants, and microapproaches based mainly on surveys (Bahna, 2008).

Existing research on social capital and migration has shown that social capital affects the migration process in various ways. In the majority of cases, social networks emerged through individual ties between close friends and relatives, or more distant acquaintances, or friends of friends, increasing opportunities for mobilizing social capital (Massey and Aysa, 2005) and creating migration social capital (Garip, 2008). By relying on material assistance, moral support or valuable information, individuals can increase their opportunities to reduce the costs and risks of migration (Massey and Aysa, 2005) and increase migration intentions. For example, individuals who have family members who are current or former migrants are more likely to migrate themselves (Pallioni *et al.*, 2001; Garip, 2008), not least because informal migration networks help migrants to finance their travel, stay, and to find a job or accommodation (Haug, 2008).

With the expansion of network ties, more social capital is likely to be accumulated and integrated in a process of "cumulative causation" (Massay, 1990). In that way, migration flows might become self-sustaining and dampen the effects of other social and economic factors on migration (Massey *et al.*, 1994; Massey and Espinosa, 1997; Dunlevy, 1991). However, it is important to acknowledge that migrant social capital resources might work differently for different groups of individuals or in different settings (Kanaiaupuni, 2000; Curran and Rivero-Fuentes, 2003; Fussell and Massey, 2004; Curran *et al.*, 2005). This mainly depends on the settings and changes in the relationships within the group over time (Garip, 2008). For example, Haug (2008) finds that location-specific social capital plays a decisive role in migration decisions – differences in social capital at the destination and place of residence affect migration decisions.

It is important to distinguish between three dimensions of migration social capital: the recipients, the sources and the resources themselves (Portes, 1998). Different information or different kinds of assistance could be available to migrants at different stages of the migration process. The recipients might then access these resources through migration networks, which are sets of interpersonal ties based on kinship, friendship, or shared community of origin, which connect migrants and nonmigrants (Massey *et al.*, 1993).

Furthermore, family reunification programmes and diaspora network connections provide valuable migration social capital resources. They can supply potential migrants with better information about destinations, such as job opportunities and housing or financial capital through remittances and investment (Adams, 2003; Kugler and Rapoport, 2007; Docquier and Lodigiani, 2010; Leblang, 2010) and various forms of "social remittances" (Levitt, 1998). These connections may provide financial aid to migrants as well as social and emotional support once in the destination country (Massey, 1990).

Many of these findings have had a strong impact on policymaking in the integration processes for migrants in a number of countries. Moreover, the concept has appeared as an important tool in policymaking for a number of international actors such as the World Bank, UNDP (United Nations Development Programme), IOM (International Organization for Migration), ILO (International Labour Organization) and other international organizations currently operating in the field of migration. Policymakers have started to take into consideration interpersonal and organizational social ties with regard to who migrates and where, the kinds of employment available to migrants in the host country and the migrants' relationship with their country of origin (Poros, 2011). At the same time, they also acknowledge that migrant social networks might work against immigrants through cultural isolation, limiting their opportunities to use coethnic resources, or promoting labour-market exploitation. However, social capital remains highly relevant to the policy discourse. This targets various initiatives of economic incorporation of immigrants, migration and development and transnational policies and practices.

However, while the effect of social capital has been examined with relation to potential and actual migrants, as well as nonmigrants who have stayed in their country of origin, little research has focused on the social capital of ex-diaspora returnees, external migrants and those who were internally displaced in a postconflict environment – the main focus of our research. While several studies have investigated each of these categories separately, there are hardly any studies that investigate potential relationships between these groups, or compare them, with regard to their social capital, both at group and individual level, examining features such as networks, entrepreneurship, trust, economy, ethnicity, gender and age. For example, Stamm (2006), in his research about migrant returnees in Lebanon, focused mainly on the importance of social networks in migrants' decisions to return to their place of origin or "home". Social networks gain a lot of attentions among researchers studying internally displaced persons (IDPs), who frequently confronted recovery programs with resources that they obtained through social relations (Aldrich, 2012).

Social Capital, Ethnic Diversity and Economic Performance

The importance of ethnicity for social capital has already been identified in the broader literature. Ethnicity represents an important feature of economic, political and social life in multicultural societies. It might play an important role in economic performance (Alesina and La Ferrara, 2005; Gonzales, 2013), economic development (Montalvo and Reynal-Querol, 2005), economic growth (Goren, 2014), business aspirations (Efendic *et al.*, 2015) and civil society (Putnam, 2007). A number of studies showed that institutions, households and individuals in diverse multiethnic societies might negotiate the category of ethnicity in different ways (Alesina and La Ferrara, 2005; Montalvo and Reynal-Querol, 2005; Putnam, 2007). On the one hand, it might lead to political unrest or civil wars, while on the other hand, it might bring innovations and creativity (Alesina and La Ferrara, 2005). That depends largely on the principles and mechanisms of democratic governance and civil institutions, free market, civil society and human rights (Putnam, 2007) and social relations and civil networks. Many researchers identify a negative relationship between ethnically fragmented societies and nondemocratic societies (Knack and Keefer, 1997) or less-developed countries (Collier, 1998). For example, Collier (2001) showed that ethnic diversity affects social capital negatively in the developing country, while a lack of democratic mechanisms creates a negative atmosphere for civil society and social relationships in general. Still, it is important to bear in mind the existence of the cross-country differences as well as the importance of the local context and everyday lives for ethnically diverse societies. For example, many studies demonstrate how the urban environment positively affects the relationships between ethnic diversity and social capital (Florida, 2002; Gates *et al.*, 2012), where the neighbourhoods with everyday interactions between people might overcome various social conflicts, including those based on ethnicity. The diversity of social capital and ethnicity is evident at various economic levels: macro, meso and micro. While ethnic diversity might affect social capital negatively at the macro level, this is frequently not the case at the lower levels of analysis.

The ambivalent relationship between ethnicity and social capital should therefore not be oversimplified. Previous studies imply that complexity – but also the importance of understanding the link between ethnicity and different dimension of social capital that we focus on (trust or relational dimension of social capital; networks or structural social capital; and prosocial actions of individuals on the ground) – as well as understanding the ethnicity itself play a key role in social capital dynamics. An overview of these studies is reported in Chapters 5 and 6.

The association between different forms of ethnic diversity and economic performance has been the focus of considerable economic research since the late 1990s, generally finding that "ethnicity does matter in economics". However, empirical research supports opposing hypotheses regarding ethnic diversity and economic performance, suggesting both positive and negative effects on outcomes as well as more-or-less strong and/or significant influences (Constant et al., 2009). This may reflect attempts to identify the economic consequences of ethnic diversity at different levels of economic analysis.

A conventional theoretical proposition in the diversity literature is that – ceteris paribus – greater ethnic diversity may increase ethnic tensions and conflicts (Osborne, 2000). In turn, ethnic conflicts or higher probabilities of ethnic conflicts have a negative impact on economic incentives and economic performance. Thus, the available literature argues that ethnic diversity, fractionalization, conflicts and prejudice can override economic incentives, leading to poor economic choices, policies, outcomes and political instability. In general, ethnically polarized societies are more likely to select suboptimal economic policies, which in turn reduce economic prosperity (Easterly and Levine, 1997). Accordingly, ethnic diversity is usually associated with poorer economic performance, reducing economic growth either directly or through indirect transmission mechanisms (Collier, 1998; Alesina and La Ferrara, 2005; Goren, 2014).

A different perspective in the literature is that most developed countries and city regions today are ethnically diverse. Proponents of this approach explain that a diverse ethnic mix may bring various abilities, different experiences, a variety of cultures and traditions, a spectrum of religious beliefs and practices and multidimensional ways of thinking, which may lead the whole society towards greater innovation, creativity and economic performance – hence, ethnic diversity might be considered as an important asset for human development and welfare (Alesina and La Ferrara, 2005; Bellini et al., 2013). Ethnic diversity might have positive consequences not only at national level but, in particular, on the economic success of regions and cities (Jacobs, 1961; Miguel et al., 2003) as well as on the productivity of individuals (Ottaviano and Peri, 2006) and, accordingly, individual wellbeing (Akerlof and Kranton, 2010).

As the main contribution of our empirical study we investigate the effect of ethnic diversity on social capital and economic performance in a society (BiH) with a recent history of ethnic conflict.[1] Ethnic conflict has changed the ethnic composition of this society with unknown social and economic consequences for individuals and households living in more-or-less homogenous or heterogeneous regions. Our literature review suggests that a good number of macroeconomic and mesoeconomic studies investigate the effect of ethnic diversity on different economic outcomes; however, this is the first research, to the best of our knowledge, which investigates the effect of ethnic diversity on individual and household incomes and for a postconflict society in particular (Chapter 6). The same observation applies to research on the role of ethnic diversity in social capital formation for different migrant categories (Chapter 5).

---

[1]   In the literature reviewed above, many authors (e.g. Alesina and La Ferrara, 2005) distinguish ethnic from linguistic and religious groups in their research and analyse these differences separately. In the context of BiH, however, there are no "real" language differences inside the country between different ethnicities. In contrast, the dominant ethnicities in BiH (Bosniacs, Serbs and Croats) largely correspond to religious differentiations (Muslims, Orthodox and Catholics respectively).

Adnan Efendic

Social Capital in Periods of Crisis and Normality – Empirical Investigation from Bosnia and Herzegovina

Introduction

Bosnia and Herzegovina (BiH) is a well-known country due, unfortunately, to the conflict, which lasted four years between 1992 and 1995 and involved ethnic violence. The war led to around 50% of its citizens being internally and externally displaced. Two decades later, reconciliation is still a salient issue. In May 2014 the country was suddenly affected with unforeseen floods, the like of which had not been seen in the modern history of this region. In one day, much of the country was under water, with landslides destroying whole villages but, surprisingly, only a few lives were lost. This was not due to a functional institutional response, which was limited by the broken public infrastructure, but, interestingly enough, it was thanks to the citizens who organized themselves in a day and managed to save endangered lives, wealth, animals and even state or private institutions. For the first time, this rather ethnically divided country witnessed the importance of its social capital; there was hope that the diverse people living there were coming together (UNDPBiH, 2009). During the flood period, "ethnic boundaries" between people seemed less relevant.

This event inspired our investigation and research questions, as BiH has been classified as a country with low levels of social capital (Hakansson and Sjoholm, 2007; UNDP, 2007, 2009; Whitt, 2010). Yet, here, during the flood crisis period, people started acting together to help out others – not just their neighbours or family, but people on the other side of the country with whom they had no relations. Thus, we are interested in investigating the similarities and difference in social capital during periods of disaster (crisis) and periods of (postcrisis) normality. To the best of our knowledge, there is no study that simultaneously investigated determinants of social capital in such two structurally different periods. In particular, we ask "to what extent do the determinants of social capital in a period of crisis and normality differ?" As we explained in our theoretical chapter, we conceptualize social capital as a multidimensional concept that can be divided into social capital outcomes and inputs. Social capital inputs are the vehicles through which social capital can be accumulated (e.g. networks and norms) and social capital outputs (e.g. prosocial actions of individuals) are the resources that can be obtained from the social relations (Grootaert *et al.*, 2004). In particular we are interested in the role of social capital inputs of networking, in terms of size and structure, and norms, in terms of trust, in producing social capital outcomes in the provision of resources by individuals, which can also be understood as prosocial behaviour in times of crisis and noncrisis.

Social Capital – A Multidimensional Construct: Inputs and Outputs

Social capital has been advanced as a crucial building block of society, which can influence institutional efficiency, economic development, crime rates and the incidence of other social and environmental problems (Lesage and Ha, 2012). A higher level of social capital is argued to improve political stability, enhance factor productivity and social integration in the very end (e.g. Knack and Keefer, 1997; Rose, 1999; Kaasa, 2009; Lesage and Ha, 2012). In this chapter we are interested in examining the relationship between social capital and the likelihood that individuals engage in prosocial behaviour in times of normality and in times of crisis.

Prosocial behaviour is action that is taken with the intention of improving the situation of another person or persons where the actor is not motivated by the fulfilment of professional obligations (Bierhoff, 2002). Research has indicated that social capital facilitates prosocial behaviour in both crisis and noncrisis periods. For example, research suggests that social capital is linked to the likelihood of an individual being a social entrepreneur in noncrisis periods (Stephan *et al.*, 2015). Social capital can play an important role in postcrisis recovery by encouraging prosocial behaviour, facilitating proactive participation by individuals and communities in recovery and rehabilitation activities and can serve as "informal insurance" during or after a disaster (Nakagawa and Shaw, 2004; Aldrich, 2010). This is important because research on societies that were recovering from disasters showed that prosocial behaviour, such as collective action, has the potential to overcome a lack of economic resources or assistance from national and international agencies and to reduce the level of damage, facilitating postcrisis recovery and reconstruction (Aldrich, 2012).

As we saw in Chapter 2 of this book, social capital has been a highly contested field of research. Definitions and conceptualizations of social capital have proliferated, stemming from a number of works that have shaped the literature of social capital (Bourdieu, 1980; Burt, 1982; Coleman, 1988). A common feature of all these views is that the core element of social capital remains relations to people, interactions and approach to resources, while the differences exist mainly in the conceptualization and interpretation of the social capital in relation to individuals, networks and social structures. Adler and Kwon (2002, p. 17) define social capital as "the goodwill that is engendered by the fabric of social relations and that can be mobilized to facilitate action." Yet, as Coleman (1990) points out, social capital is not one entity, but a variety of different entities. Thus we argue that social capital is best understood as a multidimensional and multilevel phenomenon (Grootaert *et al.*, 2004; Efendic *et al.*, 2015).

The input dimensions of social capital are often categorized into two main types: networks and norms (Coleman, 1990; Putnam, 1995; Woolcock, 1998; Grootaert *et al.*, 2004; Efendic *et al.*, 2015). The first type is often referred to as the structural dimension of social capital. Structural social capital reflects "the overall pattern of connections between actors – that is, who you reach and how you reach them" (Nahapiet and Ghoshal, 1998, p. 244), i.e. the number, types and configurations of network ties. The second is often referred to as the relational dimension of social capital or "those assets created and leveraged through relationships" (Nahapiet and Ghoshal, 1998, p. 244) – norms such as trust and expectations of trustworthy behaviour. Without going into this conceptual discussion, for the purpose of this chapter and the measures that we use later on, we will refer to Nahapiet and Ghoshal's (1988) work and their term "relational" dimension of social capital, which captures generalized and specific trust. Accordingly, we investigate the relationship between structural and relational dimensions of social capital and their effect on prosocial behaviour, which could be understood as a behaviour full of goodwill, which is facilitated by social capital (Adler and Kwon, 2002; Gootaert *et al.*, 2004). Although the existing studies sometimes cover more dimensions of social capital in their focus, including Nahapiet and Ghoshal (1988) and Gootaert *et al.* (2004), whose approaches are the most similar to that used in this research, we focus on these key dimensions as a priority for our investigation and as dimensions that are feasible to observe given the existing dataset with which we operate.

Putnam (1993) argues that in crisis periods, such as times of natural disaster, or in our case floods, social capital outputs might be affected less by some individual socio-personal characteristics like education, employment and social class, but rather pulled by increasing norms of reciprocity and networks of civic engagement. Prosocial behaviour can therefore serve as "informal insurance" during or after a disaster, overcoming social capital problems by stimulating recovery in the neighbourhood's or community-based networks (Aldrich, 2010). In normal times these elements might directly limit access to social capital given that participation in associations and networks depends largely on one's resources and social status (Sopha, 2007). To the best of our knowledge, there is no research that investigates the importance of social capital inputs, socio-economic and individual characteristics for social capital outputs (prosocial behaviour) simultaneously, both in times of crisis and normality. If these prosocial activities are not investigated simultaneously for the same actors, our understanding of their links will remain poor and policy implications will be limited. By adopting this strategy we do not accept that the prosocial activities of people in normal or crisis periods are exogenous responses, driven by independent forces but, on the contrary, these activities are coming form a joint system of influences that are linked with common factors, specific once, and thanks to our research strategy, by those being invisible and not directly controlled for.

We can understand structural social capital (networks and patterns of connections) as a social capital input (Grootaert *et al.*, 2004). Groups and networks are tools that are used to obtain knowledge and information, provide access to different types of resources and facilitate actions; they are resources that individuals use in a series of regular or emergency situations. If we accept this argument, there is a reason to include groups and networks as explanatory variables for prosocial behaviour, which is an output measure of social capital. We analyse the relationship between size of networks, membership of associations and the structure of the networks in terms of strong and weak ties and ethnic diversity.

Ethnic diversity is an important aspect of network structure in a society like BiH, which faces ethnic tensions and a lack of ethnic tolerance (Efendic *et al.*, 2015). Interethnic networking is likely to play a role in social capital outcomes (Edwards *et al.*, 2006). We know that individuals who are friends with individuals from different ethnic groups are more likely to have stronger forms of other social capital such as being parts of associations (UNDP, 2009).

We include three dimensions of relational social capital in our empirical model – trust in general people, trust in people in their municipality and trust in institutions as social capital input measures. In most of the literature, trust represents a fundamental dimension of social capital (Bourdieu, 1980, 1986; Portes, 1998; Putnam, 2000; Alder and Kwon, 2002; Grossman, 2013; Savioli and Patuelli, 2016) and individual actions are therefore shaped, redirected and constrained, among other things, by interpersonal trust, social networks and organizations (Coleman, 1988). The effect of trust on social capital outcome might be both positive and negative (Nooteboom, 2007). In the context of our model, we expect that greater trust in people might positively support social capital on the ground, while greater trust in institutions might reduce it. If greater institutional trust exists, there are higher expectations of institutional outcomes and support, which might reduce incentives for social collective action.

Sample, Survey Design, Data and Methodology

Prism Research agency for social, media and marketing research, which is active in BiH, conducted the targeted survey for this research over the period from June to August, 2015 on a sample of 6021 randomly selected respondents.[1] The sample is representative of 138 out of 143

---

1   The technique of random selection by closest birthday was used to implement the survey. On first contact, the interviewers asked about the number of persons living in one apartment or house between 16 and 65 years old. The interviewers conducted the interview with a selected household member whose birthday was closest to the

municipalities in BiH. Five municipalities did not participate in the survey because there were not enough telephone numbers available in the database. These municipalities are among the smallest ones in BiH, with only a few hundred citizens. The survey was conducted via computer-assisted telephone interviewing (CATI). It was prepared in a special survey program *The Survey System 9.0*; the telephone database used for this survey had almost one million active numbers. The survey was designed so that each municipality should have at least 40 participants but that the total number from all municipalities should be at least 6000.

Although we operate with household survey data in this study, the social capital in our case is measured through individuals (Nieminen *et al.*, 2008). The dataset that we use for empirical modelling does not have standard missing values (i.e. unfilled responses), while "Do not know" or "Refuse to answer" responses account for around 3% of the responses on average, although some questions had more of these responses. However, we believe that these percentages should not lead to substantial bias in the estimated models and we omit these observations using simple "listwise deletion".

The Dependent Variables: Social Capital Outputs

The aim of this analysis is to understand better the determinants of the output of social capital – prosocial behaviour – in periods of crisis and normality, including social capital inputs and relevant individual and socioeconomic determinants. We measure this to establish whether individuals have worked to help others in their community in a noncrisis time or in response to a crisis (such as the 2014 floods), without distinguishing whether they worked as part of a collective response or individual action.

We measure social capital outputs in a noncrisis period by asking respondents "In the last year, have you helped anyone outside of your house for free" to which they may respond YES or NO. Around 60% of respondents report that they provided some support to others for free.

---

date they are interviewing. If that person was not at home, they arranged callbacks, if possible. The software schedules the callbacks five times before omitting the number. This method ensures a random selection of respondents. In the final dataset, there are 44 observations per municipality, on average. The minimum number of observations per municipality is 40 and the maximum is 46.

Interestingly enough, entrepreneurs report the highest percentage of this kind of support (76%). The respondents who are employed either in the formal or informal sector report that in some 67% of cases they provided support to others, which is slightly more than average.

As we have already discussed briefly, the crisis period that we use as a reference period was the flood period in BiH, which occurred between 13 and 18 May 2014, when a large part of the country was flooded for a week, with hundreds of landslides spreading damage across urban and rural areas. The public infrastructure was broken in a day, formal institutions collapsed and hundreds of thousands of citizens were forced from their homes.

To ascertain social capital outputs during a crisis period we ask respondents: "During the floods in 2014, were you involved in any activity to help the affected area?" The number of respondents who were active in supporting people affected by the floods was higher than in the previous question about social capital outputs in normal times. Around 70% of respondents reported that they provided some support and the percentage was the highest for entrepreneurs (83%). This is a good indication that prosocial behaviour in the period of crisis was high among ordinary citizens but particularly among entrepreneurs and that it was higher than in normal times.

We do not think that respondents confused their support in the crisis period (very specifically linked to floods) with the normal, typical support they provide in their neighbourhood because the floods were some two months earlier before the period covered by the question on typical support outside the family.

We also asked respondents what they did during the floods in 2014 because there were a number of ways in which citizens could support the affected areas. The majority of respondents (48%) sent or provided clothes, food, clean water and similar assistance; 31% of respondents were sending or providing money, while the rest were participating in their local community activities or going directly to these areas and volunteering. It is difficult to make a hierarchy of these different actions; in particular, it is hard to distinguish what was more important at that moment – to send some money, or water, or food, or clothes, or being there and helping. Different areas needed all these different forms of support – some areas were left without drinking water (other did not need it at all); in some areas people lost their homes and everything that go with them (they needed food, clothes and money); some were stuck in mud and only needed direct assistance with cleaning. However, this support was something that was linked to the sudden crisis in the country and we argue that it is important to investigate if this dimension of social capital – prosocial action and cooperation – differed from the prosocial activities of individuals in typical, noncrisis times. Figure 3.1 plots the mean values at the municipal level of social capital outputs in normal and crisis time in BiH to create a heat map.

Coloured municipalities that have a mean value of social capital output between 0.8 and 1.0 are red, indicating that between 80% to 100% of the population has participated in that form of prosocial action. Orange municipalities have a mean that lies between 0.6 to 0.8; yellow 0.4 to 0.6; green 0.2 to 0.4 and blue 0.2 and below. The maps clearly show that average levels of social capital output varied across municipalities as we see the colour of the map ranges from green to red. It also shows that in many municipalities social capital outputs are more prevalent in a period of crisis than for the noncrisis period.

Social capital in the crisis time	Social capital in the normal postcrisis time

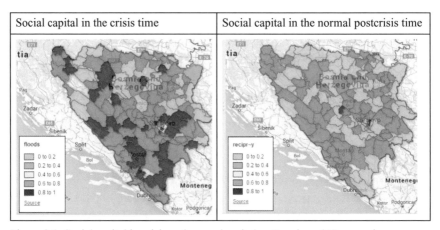

Figure 3.1: Social capital in crisis and normal periods – Bosnia and Herzegovina.

These figures also indicate that higher levels of social capital outcomes are not geographically clustered in particular areas. This is interesting because it indicates that, during the flood period, when floods affected certain parts of the country, the engagement of citizens was not linked to these regions but was prevalent in all parts of the country.

Independent Variables

Next we turn to our measures of structural and relational social capital – input elements of social capital that we hypothesize will explain the propensity of individuals to take part in prosocial actions. The first dimension of social capital that we discuss here is trust, or relational social capital. This category includes three types of trust: trust in unknown people – generalized trust; trust towards local people – municipal trust; and trust in the government – institutional trust. The trust variables are almost standard in the literature as key dimensions of social capital (Kwon and Arenius, 2010; Westlund and Adam, 2010) and have a long history in empirical studies focusing on relational social capital. We replicated questions from existing studies (for generalized trust we rely on the World Value Survey questions; for institutional trust we replicated questions from Efendic *et al.*, 2011, 2015) but use a wider scale of responses identified as important through our piloting procedure. If we examine general trust in people (*gentrust*), we can see that over 80% of respondents report that they "need to be very careful" with people in general, which suggests that the general level of trust in that society is low. There is a little more trust in local people than people in general but still the percentage of those who think that they should be careful is very high (75%). Overall, these descriptive statistics provide enough information to lead to a conclusion that the general level of trust in this society is very low.

The next category of trust that we examine is institutional trust (*insttrust*)– confidence in institutions at different administrative levels in BiH (national, entity and municipal), based on earlier literature on institutional trust in this country (Efendic *et al.*, 2011, 2015).[2] The responses included a scale from 1 (very little confidence) to 5 (a lot of confidence). Around 60% of the respondents reported that they have very little confidence in these different institutional levels. There is a little more confidence in local authorities (a few percentage points more), although the

---

2   Bosnia and Herzegovina has three administrative levels, including state level, entity level and municipal level. The term "state government" refers to what would be considered the national or federal government in other federal systems; "entity governments" are analogous to "state or provincial governments" in other federal systems and "municipal level" includes municipalities as in other countries. In addition to this, one entity (Federation BiH) has a meso-administrative level, cantons or cantonal governments, which are a sort of provincial government. However, as this level exists only in one entity we have omitted it from our descriptive statistics.

main conclusion still applies. The scale of responses is the same for trust in people, but there is slightly more trust in institutions than in people in general, which is an interesting finding.

The structural dimension of social capital captures information on group membership, the scope of the network and the internal diversity of network membership (Grootaert *et al.*, 2004). Based on this, we investigated whether respondents were "a member of any group linked to sports, music, arts, political party, NGO, professional and business association, charity, etc." The respondents could answer this questions with YES (having two further possibilities – being active or inactive), or with NO. The majority of respondents were not active in the groups listed in our question, whereas 13% of them were members in a group (*group*).

Next, we analysed the size and structure of the networks in which people were involved in their everyday-life activities. Firstly, we asked respondents the following question: "On average, about how many people do you have contact with in a typical day including all those you chat, talk or discuss matters with, whether you do it face to face, by telephone, by mail or via the Internet and whether you personally know the person or not?" The majority of respondents reported that their network size was in the range of 5–20 people (*contsized*).

As we have already pointed out, it is important to investigate not only the size but also the structure of a network (*ethncont*). The database gives us the opportunity to analyse the internal diversity of membership based on family, friends, acquaintances and other participants. The respondents reported approximate percentages for these four types of members in their networks. The results indicate dominance of family and friends – on average, 57% of networks are composed of family members while 47% are linked to friends. Acquaintances and other members take 36% and 31% respectively. Accordingly, the networks have a structure that is based more on strong ties rather than weak ones.

The next important issue for a structure of network in the postconflict context is the ethnic composition of networks. This information has already been identified as important in research focused on this region (Efendic *et al.*, 2015). We asked respondents what percentage of their network members belong to other ethnicities. Bosnia and Herzegovina is a multi-ethnic environment having three dominant ethnicities and more homogenous or heterogeneous networks can have different effects on social capital outcomes. To the best of our knowledge, this issue has not been addressed in the literature. However, the mean value in our sample is 12%, while some 45% of respondents report ethnically homogenous networks. This suggests that there is more ethnic homogeneity in the networks than diversity, on average. Although this question is rather interesting for our investigation, one of its limitations is that it produced some 24% of responses that were "do not wish/refuse" to answer, which reduced our sample in empirical modelling. This is not surprising as any ethnic-related question in this country can be considered as sensitive.

We investigated the relationships between the different input dimensions of social capital to check whether our measures of social capital should be treated as multidimensional and not as single factors. Factor analysis and Cronbach's alpha suggest that the creation of one composite indicator of social capital is not advisable, thus supporting the argument that the different dimensions of social capital should be considered separately. This result that we obtained in this regard was consistent with the existing literature (e.g. Stone and Hughes, 2002; Grootaert *et al.*, 2004; van der Gaag and Snijders, 2005; Nieminen *et al.*, 2008), which reports the complexity of social capital measurement, concludes that social capital is a multidimensional phenomenon and suggests dividing social capital into three dimensions.

Table 3.1 presents descriptive statistics of the variables used in our empirical investigation. Note that, for reasons of space, we omit descriptive statistics and more detailed discussion of other determinants used in the empirical model.

Table 3.1 Descriptive statistics of the main variables of interest.

Variables	Description of variables	Number of obser- vations	Mean	Do not knows/ na (%)
Social capital outputs				
normality	Helping others for free in the last year: 0 = no; 1 = yes	5963	0.61	1.0
crisis	Helping others during the floods: 0 = no; 1 = yes	5981	0.70	0.7
Social capital inputs				
group	Member of any group: 0 = No; 1 = Yes	5997	0.13	0.4
contsized	Size of the networks: 0 = 0–9 persons; 1 = 10 and over	5144	0.55	14.6

Variables	Description of variables	Number of obser- vations	Mean	Do not knows/ na (%)
ethncont	Other ethnicities in network: 0% to 100%	4566	12.23	24.2
strongtie	Strong networks – family, friends: 0 = min to 50 = max	4626	36.90	23.2
weaktie	Weak – acquaintances, other: 0 = min to 50 = max (base)	4626	13.10	23.2
gentrust	Generalized trust in people: 0 = no trust; 1 = trust	5853	1.36	2.9
muntrust	Generalized trust in local people: 0 = no trust; 1 = trust	5807	1.57	3.6
*insttrust**	Institutional trust: 0 = no trust; 1 = trust	5284	1.69	12.2
Sociodemographic characteristics				
age	Age of respondents: 16 to 65 years	6021	47.10	0.0
male	Gender: 0 = female; 1 = male	6021	0.45	0.0
educat	Education: 0 = no and primary; 1 = second- ary and high	5993	0.71	0.5
femploy	Employed in formal sector: 0 = no; 1 = yes	6004	0.27	0.3
infemploy	Employed in informal sector: 0 = no; 1 = yes	5996	0.26	0.5
outoflabour	Outside of the labour force: 0 = no; 1 = yes	6021	0.38	0.0
incomeper	Personal income: 0 = below average; 1 = average/above	5164	0.49	14.3
urban	Urban area: 0 = no; 1 = yes	6021	0.28	0.0
suburban	Suburban area: 0 = no; 1 = yes	6021	0.24	0.0
rural	Rural area: 0 = no; 1 = yes (base category)	6021	0.48	0.0
fbih	Entity in BiH: 0 = other; 1 = federation BiH	6021	0.57	0.0
rsbih	Entity in BiH: 0 = other; 1 = Republika Srpska	6021	0.42	0.0
dbbih	Entity in BiH: 0 = other; 1 = District of Brcko (base)	6021	0.01	0.0
mixed	Self-declared ethnicity: 0 = other; 1 = mixed	5831	0.31	3.2

Note: *The variable *insttrust* is a factor variable, which includes an aggregation of trust in insti- tutions at the national, entity and municipality levels. The factor analysis and Cronbach's alpha analysis supported this strategy.

Empirical Procedure and Analysis

Our empirical investigation is guided by theoretical reasoning and by the argument that social capital is a multidimensional phenomenon and that a single indicator that can measure social capital is not appropriate. Indeed, our initial investigation has confirmed that having one aggregated proxy for social capital is not a feasible strategy. Accordingly, we focus our attention on relational social capital (trust), structural social capital (groups and networks) and prosocial activities of citizens (actions of individuals in typical periods and crisis periods) as three dimensions of social capital in our main focus. If we start with these three dimensions of social capital, the main challenge becomes how to establish causal relations between them because they might appear as both outputs and inputs of social capital. Accordingly, there is a need to think carefully about causal relations as well as potential problems of endogeneity in empirical modelling.

Our empirical specifications will include prosocial behaviours – both in the normal period (*normality*) and in the crisis period (*crisis*) – as the dependent variable(s) measuring this social capital's output dimensions. We believe that the activities of individuals on the ground are the best proxies for social capital outcomes in this society. Investigating similarities and differences of social capital activities in a typical period and a crisis period means that reciprocity might be systematically affected by different social capital inputs and individual and socioeconomic determinants (Putnam, 1993). In the model that we use, social capital inputs, which appear as independent variables, include membership in groups and associations (*group*) and networks in terms of size (*contsized)* and structure *(strongtie, ethncont)*. We controlled for typical structures of networks in the context of strong and weak ties (*strongtie*), which is an appropriate approach to the structure of networks, in particular in the business literature (e.g. Greve and Salaff, 2003; Efendic *et al.*, 2015). Linked to the sample that we examined we included two more network structures to be explored. Firstly, this is a postconflict environment that inherited a number of ethnically related problems and tensions. More than two decades after the war, the country still remains segregated along ethnic lines, while the three dominant ethnic groups (Bosniacs, Serbs and Croats) have substantial autonomy and control over their own ethnoterritorial units (Bieber, 2010). In such an environment, people rely on networks, which might be more or less ethnically homogenous, often reflecting ethnic diversity at the local level. Accordingly, we controlled the ethnic structure of these networks according to whether they were more or less ethnically diverse (*ethcont*) and its association to the social capital activities on the ground (i.e. our dependent variables).

There is an issue that social capital inputs may also be affected by social capital outputs (prosocial behaviour). While membership in groups and the size and structure of networks could explain prosocial behaviour, membership in groups and networks might be encouraged by this prosocial behaviour as well. However, we believe that this is a less likely scenario, especially in the context of formal membership in different groups, which does not happen over the course of a few days. Networks are built over time and inherited mainly from the past. As Efendic *et al.* (2015) pointed out, it is less likely that networks change over short period of time in postconflict and low-trust societies. We believe that networks used in everyday life and especially in the period of crisis were inherited from the past and they were used to support collective actions in the short run, but not the other way around.

Relational social capital (i.e. trust questions) is more problematic to model because it appears in the literature as an input but also as an output measure of social capital. Still the main challenge that we have in our dataset is that this variable has very little variation – the responses in our case are fully left-hand skewed. Over 80% of respondents answered trust questions by choosing the lowest rank on the scale. There is a probably a need to establish better measures of trust in postconflict societies, while in our case we need to accept that there was really low trust in people and institutions. However, this is something that needs to be addressed in the future research. In the context of our model, for statistical reasons (potential misspecification bias), we include these variables in the model as input measures. We believe that having trust in people and institutions might explain social actions on the ground, especially in the periods of crisis when institutions collapsed, being blocked or at least limited in their operation.

In addition to the different social capital dimensions in the model, we included some more specific determinants linked to individuals, households and the postconflict context. Firstly, we controlled for typical individual characteristics as explanatory variables, namely age of respondents (*age*), gender (*male*), level of education (*educat*), type of geographic area in which they lived (*urban, suburban, rural* and regions: *fbih, rsbih, dbbih*) and type of ethnic composition of the area (*mixed* or not). We expected that respondents who were older, male, more educated and from urban area would report more social activities. However, the effects of these individual characteristics might have different directions (positive or negative). As a postconflict ethnic influence in the model and based on earlier findings for the business literature (Efendic *et al.*, 2015), we expect that respondents having more ethnically diverse networks (*mixed*) might have more social capital outputs in periods of crisis and normality.

Next, we controlled economic characteristics of respondents, which could also be relevant in explaining social capital outcomes. We controlled for the employment status of respondents, distinguishing between formal (*femploy*) and informal employment (*infemploy*). One of the characteristics of BiH's economy is extremely high official unemployment (45%) and the presence of a large "grey" economy. Every social interaction that we observe, including prosocial behaviour, incurs some costs, which need to be financed by the actors (Marmaros and Sacerdote, 2006) and in the context of our investigation it is important to control for the effect of employment as the main source of income, including formal and informal employment. As a huge proportion of population is earning some income in the informal economy and from unofficial sources, our strategy should capture the specific socioeconomic environment of this postconflict society. With such an approach it gains validity. Indeed, in our sample 34% or respondents reported having informal jobs or activities that brought them some income.

After presenting the main variables used in the modelling procedure, our next step is to estimate two separate probit models (explaining social capital output in two periods in focus). Both models have appropriate model diagnostics in terms of their goodness of fit, which was the initial step in our checking procedure. Next, we look at the results – in general, we find that there is a lot of similarity but also some differences between determinants effecting social actions of individuals in the typical period and the crisis period (Table 3.3, Models 1 and 2). In order to compare the difference between the estimated coefficients in the two estimated probit models, our further check was to test if this difference is systematic (i.e.

statistically significant).[3] As we can see, there is a structural difference between the estimated coefficients between the two models for variables capturing membership in groups (*group*), age (*age*), gender (*male*), formal and informal employment (*femploy, infemploy*). The first interesting result is for gender. There is a significant difference in the way that female respondents were much more socially active in the period of crisis in comparison to the period of normality in comparison to males. Formal employment was important in influencing the response in the period of crisis, while informal employment was more relevant for social capital activities in normal times, which suggest that these different types of employment have different effects on social capital outcomes in different circumstances.

Different decisions and social capital activities are implemented by the same individuals and one would expect that these actions are outcomes from the same system (which is in this case particular individual), hence, they might be linked through these observed determinants (already identified and discussed in our modelling procedure), but more importantly, through some complex unobserved determinants not available for modelling. In line with this, we do not interpret these results as final but go a step further and estimate an endogenous model, which controls not only for observed determinants (which are part of our model specification) but also for unobserved endogenous influences in the system (which are part of the error term). A model that has such statistical properties is the system of regression equations estimated as the seemingly unrelated bivariate probit model (SUPM).

The SUPM is a system of equations in which the error terms are allowed to be correlated between equations (Gould *et al.*, 2006), while common observed determinants are included in both regressions. The SUPM allows for a more complex ("seemingly unrelated") pattern of joint determinations than "simple" simultaneity. Hence, the relationship between respondents' social activities in the typical period and in the

---

3   The procedure for testing the difference in the estimated coefficients between the two
     equations (Model 1 and Model 2) was as follows. First, we run the two probit regres-
     sions separately and stored the results of each model. Then we used the *suest* command
     in STATA 14 to estimate these two models simultaneously. We used the *test* command
     to make comparisons of the coefficients between the two models (comparing the coef-
     ficients between the groups) and we compared each variable between the two models.
     The null hypothesis is that the estimated coefficients between the two equations are not
     structurally different.

crisis period is modelled implicitly through the unobserved correlations in the error terms (Heij *et al.*, 2004), as well as explicitly by controlling for common observable variables in the system. Given that there can be unob-served factors that influence social activities in typical and crisis periods at the same time, SUPM is an appropriate methodology for our model. Even though in most cases "neither model is perfectly correct" (Roodman, 2009, p. 22), this mode of linkage comes closer to representing the "com-plex" relationship between different dimensions of social capital.

We estimate a SUPM as follows:

$$normality_1 = \hat{\beta}_1 + X_K \cdot \hat{\beta}_{1,k} + \hat{u}_1 \qquad (3.1)$$

$$crisis_2 = \hat{\beta}_2 + X_K \cdot \hat{\beta}_{2,k} + \hat{u}_2 \qquad (3.2)$$

$$\hat{\rho} = Cov(\hat{u}_1, \hat{u}_2) \qquad (3.3)$$

To simplify specifications, we do not index the (cross-section) obser-vations. In Equation (3.1) (index$_1$), *normality*$_1$ denotes the respondent's activities over the last 12 months; while in Equation (3.2) (index $_2$) *crisis*$_2$ codes the respondent's activity in the period of floods – crisis period. $\hat{\beta}_1$ and $\hat{\beta}_2$ are the intercepts in the first and second equations respectively; $\hat{\beta}_{1,k}, \hat{\beta}_{2,k}, \hat{\beta}_{1,A}, \hat{\beta}_{2,B}$ are vectors of coefficients to be estimated ($k \times 1$, $A \times 1$ and $B \times 1$ respectively); X_K is a $1 \times k$ vector of k variables that appear in both equations. $\hat{u}_1$ and $\hat{u}_2$ are potentially correlated error terms in the first and second equations respectively and contain unobserved influences that may contribute to the joint determination of two different social capital out-comes. In Equation (3.3), the parameter $\hat{\rho}$ can be interpreted as the correla-tion between the unobservable explanatory variables of the two equations (Fabbri *et al.*, 2004). In order to clarify the relationships to be estimated, Figure 3.2 provides a visual depiction of the model.

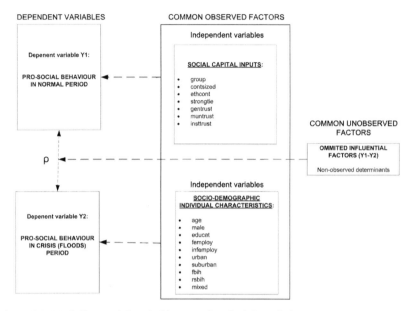

Figure 3.2: Modelling social capital in normal and crisis periods.

A particular feature of this "seemingly unrelated regressions" framework is that it takes into account and measures the correlation between the unobserved influences on the two dependent variables. Accordingly, the estimated model will enable us to test the coefficient from this endogenous system validity with three possible outcomes:

- social capital activities in typical and crisis time are not associated in the manner suggested by this model; hence, they are exogenous and should be estimated separately.
- typical and crisis period social activities are endogenously associated in one of two ways:
    - social capital activities in the typical period are associated with more social capital activities in the crisis period; or
    - social capital activities in the typical period are associated with fewer social capital activities in the crisis period.

When analysing survey data, it is important to take the survey design into account. The data were collected using cluster sampling to ensure that individuals in all municipalities were represented in the data. Due to this sampling approach it is necessary to correct standard errors because individuals within the same municipality are likely to have more similarities with each other than with those outside of their municipality. This implies that error terms within clusters will not be independent of each other and we need to use cluster-robust standard errors to ensure that standard errors are not biased.

In Table 3.2 we report results from SUPM model estimated as a cluster-robust model, a model in which clusters are defined as municipalities.

Table 3.2 Results from the baseline SUPM model (cluster-robust inference).

Variable	Typical period activity				Crisis period activity			
	Coeff.	*Robust SE*	*z-stat.*	*P>|t|*	*Coeff.*	*Robust SE*	*z-stat.*	*P>|t|*
group	0.24	0.07	3.33	0.001	0.42	0.08	5.53	0.000
contsized	0.14	0.05	2.92	0.003	0.12	0.05	2.45	0.014
ethncont	0.01	0.01	3.35	0.001	0.01	0.01	2.11	0.034
strongtie	−0.01	0.01	−1.81	0.071	−0.01	0.01	−0.16	0.870
gentrust	0.08	0.09	0.96	0.338	−0.06	0.09	−0.76	0.446
muntrust	−0.05	0.07	−0.71	0.479	0.03	0.07	0.44	0.663
insttrust	0.01	0.06	0.03	0.974	0.07	0.06	1.17	0.241
age	−0.01	0.01	−2.70	0.007	0.01	0.01	1.22	0.224
male	0.06	0.05	1.24	0.214	−0.27	0.05	−5.42	0.000
educat	0.18	0.06	2.78	0.005	0.30	0.07	4.59	0.000
femploy	0.03	0.06	0.61	0.539	0.26	0.06	4.57	0.000
infemploy	0.26	0.05	4.82	0.000	0.02	0.06	0.29	0.774
urban	0.05	0.06	0.85	0.394	0.28	0.07	3.86	0.000
suburban	0.02	0.06	0.34	0.737	0.07	0.06	1.02	0.309
fbih	0.04	0.04	0.96	0.338	0.35	0.05	7.84	0.000
rsbih	−0.03	0.05	−0.65	0.518	0.24	0.05	4.59	0.000
mixed	−0.01	0.06	−0.19	0.852	−0.04	0.05	−0.90	0.366
cons	0.01	0.15	0.04	0.964	−0.49	0.15	−3.31	0.001
MODEL DIAGNOSTICS								
Number of observations	3457							
Coefficient of correlation in the residuals	$\hat{\rho} = 0.17$							
The likelihood-ratio test of $\hat{\rho} = 0$	z = 5.08; Prob >|z|= 0.000							
The Wald test for joint significance	$\chi^2(38) = 878$; Prob > χ^2 = 0.000							

Notes: The dependent variable in the first equation: *normality* (0 = not helping others; 1 = helping others for free). The dependent variable in the second equation: *crisis* (0 = not helping; 1 = helping during the floods).

Source: Author's calculations using STATA 14 (STATA 14, StataCorp, Texas, United States).

The Wald test for the joint significance of the explanatory variables rejects the null hypothesis that the explanatory variables are jointly equal to zero (p = 0.000). Of particular interest is the likelihood-ratio (LR) test of the null hypothesis $\hat{\rho} = 0$ (in other words that the unobserved influences on the right-hand side of Equation (3.3) – captured by $\hat{u}_1$ and $\hat{u}_2$ – are not correlated). This also provides a statistical test of the validity of the estimated model. This test coefficient indicates whether the SUPM is an appropriate estimator for the relationships between two types of social capital outcomes or whether the model could be estimated with two independent binary probit equations.

The p-value of the coefficient measuring the correlation between the equation unobservables is 0.000. This coefficient is statistically significant at the highest conventional level, so we reject the null hypothesis of zero correlation and the inference that estimation by separate probit equations is a better strategy. According to the positive correlation coefficient ($\hat{\rho} = 0.17$), the two dependent variables in Equation (3.3) are both determined by unobserved influences that are positively correlated across the two equations. Hence, the general finding of this model is that more social capital activities in the typical or normal period was positively and highly (0.17) correlated with more social capital in the period of crisis. This relationship is endogenously driven by unobserved influences in the model and hence from the same system – and needs to be examined in that context.

However, the coefficients that we reported in Table 3.2 are not useful for interpretation, as they are estimated as the log of the odds. We need to consider the two equations together – which is possible with SUPM. We investigate the estimated marginal effects of each variable on the probability that individuals will report having more social capital in the typical period and in the crisis period (when *normality* = 1 and *crisis* = 1). These marginal effects for the baseline model are reported in Table 3.3 (Model 3), together with marginal effects obtained from separate probit models (Models 1 and 2).

Table 3.3 Social activities of individuals in typical and crisis periods (marginal effects).

	Normal period: probit model – exogenous (Model 1)	Crisis period: probit model – exogenous (Model 2)	Test for difference of the estimated coefficients – Model 1 and Model 2	Joint effects SUPM 1 Base (Model 3)	SUPM 3 (+ income) (Model 4)
Variables	*dy/dx*	*dy/dx*	*p-values*	*dy/dx*	*dy/dx*
Social capital inputs – relational and structural dimensions variables					
group	0.09***	0.13***	0.045**	0.15***	0.14***
contsized	0.07***	0.05***	0.688	0.08***	0.06***
ethncont	0.01***	0.01*	0.344	0.01***	0.01***
strongtie	0.01**	0.01	0.114	0.01	−0.01
gentrust	0.04	−0.03	0.097*	0.01	0.01
muntrust	−0.02	0.01	0.288	−0.01	−0.01
insttrust	0.01	0.03	0.287	0.02	0.02
Socio-demographic characteristics					
age	0.01***	0.01	0.003***	0.01**	−0.01***
male	0.02	−0.10***	0.000***	−0.04**	−0.05***
educat	0.07***	0.09***	0.195	0.10***	0.09***
femploy	0.01	0.08***	0.002***	0.05***	0.01
infemploy	0.10***	0.01	0.001***	0.07***	0.07***
rrban	0.01	0.08***	0.004***	0.06***	0.06***
suburban	0.01	0.02	0.590	0.01	0.02
fbih	0.03	0.13	0.462	0.10***	0.09***
rsbih	−0.01	0.08	0.520	0.04***	0.03*
mixed	0.01	−0.02	0.494	−0.01	−0.01
incomeper	–	–	–	–	0.07***
Number of observations	3469	3480	–	3457	3079
Predicted probability	0.65	0.73	–	0.50	0.49

Note: Significance: *** 1%; ** 5%; * 10%.

As we can see, there are a number of significant variables explaining social capital outcomes in both the typical and crisis periods. We start with dimensions of social capital inputs that are relevant in the baseline model.

- Group membership appears to be the most important dimension of social capital that contributes to social capital both in the typical period and in the crisis period. There is 15% higher probability that individuals who are members of any group linked to sport, music, religion and similar are systematically engaging in more social capital activities than those who are not members of any group.
- Network size is also an important factor for social capital activities in the normal period and crisis period. There is around 8% probability that those who have bigger networks will be more supportive to others in the typical period and crisis period. Hence, network size is positively associated with social capital activities.
- Ethnic diversity of networks has a positive effect in the model suggesting that those who report ethnically more diverse networks are engaged in more social capital outcomes. This finding confirms that ethnic diversity is beneficial for social capital even in areas where the conflict had an ethnic background. Accordingly, supporting reconciliation in this society is an investment in social capital as well. However, this effect is not high (1%).
- The distinction between strong and weak ties appears significant only in the exogenous model in the normal period. Accordingly, individuals who have more weak ties are more socially active in comparison to those who have established strong ties, but in normal times only.
- As we expected, the trust questions are not significant in any model. This is linked to the concern that a lack of variation in the trust data might be the reason for the nonsignificance of any of these variables.

Accordingly, as a general conclusion we identify the importance of structural social capital – both in terms of size of the network and ethnic diversity – but there is not really a significant effect of relational social capital proxied by trust in people and institutions.

After explaining the effect of different social capital inputs in the model, we move on to the interpretation of the remaining determinants:

- The estimated effects of individual characteristics suggests that older and female respondents report more social capital activities than younger and males. The effect of gender is 4% in the baseline model, although in the model that includes the crisis data this effect is 10%, suggesting systematically greater engagement of women. More educated individuals report more social capital and having rather high marginal effect in the model (10%). Consequently, more education is beneficial for the social capital activities of the population. This effect was particularly high in the crisis period.

- The economic background of respondents produces some interesting results. Respondents who are engaged in the informal sector of the economy report a 7% higher probability of having more social capital activities than those who are not employed or who are outside the labour force. Similarly, formal employment increases this probability by 5%. A further check was made to control for the effect of personal income (Model 4), which is likely to be an endogenous variable in the model (that is why we do not include it in the baseline model). However, if we include the level of personal income in the specification, the marginal effect of income is around 7%, while formal employment status loses its significance. Obviously, these variables are capturing similar information – formal employment is a good proxy for personal income. However, informal employment does not change at all. Apparently, formal employment tends to be important in providing the resources for social capital activities (in particular in crisis period, Model 2), while informal employment is not affected by the income effect.

- Finally, respondents from urban areas report more social capital activities (6%) than those from urban or suburban areas.

The effect of ethnic structure of the surveyed areas was nonsignificant. We will not discuss the effects of regions in the model (*fbih, rsbih versus dbih*), which are included for statistical purposes.

Overall, the models reported reveal that the group membership and size were the most important determinants of social capital inputs, together with (higher) education and employment status. Structural dimensions of social capital inputs in terms of networking have the highest effect in the model. However, economic determinants should not be ignored. The formal and informal economic environment explains social capital activities, where participation in formal economy is more relevant to social capital as a source of income, while informal activity is not affected by financial background.

In the next stage we consider the effect of different determinants in the model by combining them and investigating how they work as interactions in comparison to their separate individual effects. This will enable us to identify if different combinations of input dimensions of social capital affect social capital outcomes on the ground. We estimate three-way interactions by augmenting the preferred specification from the baseline model with both the two-way and three-way interactions. We use the full sample in these estimates, which are adjusted for multiple comparisons using the Bonferroni method (StataCorp, 2011). This methodology gives us a statistically valid identification of effects from the interaction of these variables and takes account of a rich variety of direct and indirect influences (Efendic *et al.*, 2014b). The results reported below are obtained at the highest level of statistical significance.

The general view that we obtain by interacting different social capital inputs is that these inputs have important effects in the model not only in isolation but also in different combinations. Moreover, the effect of social capital inputs increased when it was combined with more dimensions. For example, while membership in groups increases social capital outputs by 15% and networking by 5%; if we combine these two input dimensions of social capital their marginal effect increases to 21% (group members with larger networks versus nonmembers with small networks). Hence there is a synergy effect when different dimensions of social capital are combined.

Additional interesting results are obtained when we combine type of employment (formal versus informal) with level of personal income. In both cases formal and informal employment combined with higher income increases marginal coefficients but the effect is higher when informal employment is combined with higher income (22%) in comparison to formal employment and higher income (14%). This result also suggests that better economic performance is associated with more social capital activities. However, in the context of the type of employment, informal employment in combination with higher income produces higher synergy than formal employment and higher income.

To check the stability of our results we estimated parsimonious models in which we excluded those variables that were not statistically significant in the main model, including trust variables and later variables measuring formal employment and ethnicity. In all these cases the main results are fully consistent in terms of statistical significance and signs and with identical or very similar magnitudes. The coefficient measuring endogenous correlations between the two equations was also statistically significant at the highest level in all estimates, with a very similar effect size (0.15). When we exclude all these variables, the effective sample size increases to 3,723 observations.

Finally, we would like to mention a few limitations of this study. Firstly, measuring and modelling social capital is a challenging task. Although the estimated models should come closer to explaining the reality of social capital, the complexity of social capital investigation leaves us with some concerns – in particular, appropriate measuring of social capital inputs and outputs taking into account potential problem of endogeneity caused by simultaneity and reverse causation. Moreover, we controlled a number of factors in our model but still there is some concern about specification bias and a need to take into account more input dimensions of social capital or better measures of some dimensions used in the model (relational social capital – i.e., trust questions).

Although we have identified a good number of determinants that explain what is happening on the ground, we must still conclude that unobservable factors are important as well. Statistically, their effect is taken into account in obtaining the outcomes but more research is needed to unpack everything that we do not know about social capital activities in postconflict societies.

Conclusion

The results regarding the social capital activities of respondents during the typical period and the crisis period indicate that these two types of activities are joint outcomes of a wider system of observed and unobserved endogenous influences. They are positively correlated; hence, more social activities in the typical period are linked with more engagement in the period of crisis. Although this outcome is reasonable, it sends a message that building social capital in the normal time or everyday life is an investment for a more secure positive response from citizens when the society is confronted with sudden challenges and crises. And this is something that societies will always need.

The observed determinants in the model reveal that social capital outcomes are strongly influenced by different social capital inputs. In particular, membership in different social groups, more networking with people and more religious activities explain prosocial activities on the ground. In the context of network structure, we find that the ethnic diversity of networks, which is particularly relevant in ethnically mixed societies, is beneficial for social engagement. Hence, ethnic tolerance is positively associated with social capital outcomes in this postconflict society. It is beneficial for growth aspirations of young companies (Efendic *et al.*, 2015) and, in the end, it is beneficial for individual and household economic performance (Chapter 6). Accordingly, in postethnic conflict societies such as BiH, investing in and supporting ethnic diversity and ethnic tolerance have multidimensional benefits for society and for individuals living in it.

There are more social activities among female respondents, as well as among more educated individuals. Informal economic activities are systematically linked with more social capital, while formal employment is also important, but primarily it works as a financial intermediary for supporting social capital activities. While having a huge grey economy has number of economic and social disadvantages, it affects social capital formation positively.

BOJANA BABIC

Social Capital and Migration – A Qualitative Investigation from the SEE Region

Introduction

The main goal of this chapter is to analyse the determinants of social capital among migrants in Bosnia and Herzegovina (BiH) and in the neighbouring countries of Serbia and Croatia. More precisely, the aim is to identify and investigate the main determinants – including economic, postconflict, ethnic, religious and individual factors – that influence the social capital of individuals differentiated by their migration status in a postconflict environment.

The three groups on which this research focuses are external migrants (ex-diaspora returnees to BiH and BiH external migrants to Serbia and Croatia), internal migrants (internally displaced persons or IDPs in BiH and those who permanently settled outside of their original municipalities) and the remaining base category consists of nonmigrants (domicile population in BiH). In addition to BiH, the inclusion of Serbia and Croatia is important due to a high percentage of BiH (e)migrants who settled there (around 300 000).[1] According to official statistics from the government of the Republic of Serbia, the number of BiH migrants in Serbia is close to 8% of the BiH population.[2] A similar population trend in this regard can be observed in Croatia (around 200 000[3] BiH migrants) with around 5% of BiH population residing there. Apart from these statistics, the two countries might offer different structural aspects of social capital in relation to peoples' experiences of migration and the political-economic environment. The findings from the project described here broaden our

---

1   Republički zavod za statistiku Srbije, 2011.
2   Ibid.
3   Državni zavod za statistiku Hrvatske, 2011.

understanding of social capital in the postconflict regions of south-eastern European (SEE) region.

Theoretical Framework

Social capital has had an important role in the (re)integration of migrants in postconflict environments in the SEE region. Studies have indicated that various programs and initiatives from national and international actors have frequently been replaced by people's own networks and ties in BiH (Valenta and Ramet, 2011). The failure of international interventions to provide livelihoods in postconflict environments was seen as being due to their focus on structural issues rather than on people's needs. This has been exacerbated by the political and socioeconomic environment, which is unfavourable for the sustainable (re)integration of the migrant and refugee population (see for example De Andrade and Delaney, 2001; Ito, 2001; Stefansson, 2004; Philpott, 2005; Jansen, 2011). Personal networks and connections at the individual, family or community level have consequently become important features of everyday life for those with different migration experiences and those without any migration experience. Moreover, people have been maintaining their livelihoods and wellbeing through social networks and ties built on various features such as their personal characteristics (ethnicity, religion, class, education and age), geographic location (rural, semiurban, urban), different migrant experiences (refugees, internally displaced persons, labour migrants, nonmigrants) and feelings of belonging.

Several studies have also pointed to the importance of locality and local belonging in the (re)construction of social networks and everyday lives of populations with different migrant status (Halilovich, 2013a). Social networks based on local belonging have served not only to increase new forms of social ties but also to recover those from prewar times (Capo and Halilovich, 2013). For instance, this social trend was found in Janja, a small return community near Bijeljina, where the sustainable return of 3000 war-displaced persons happened due to the recovery of prewar local ties and trust within the neighbourhood (Petrovic, 2007). Other studies also consider the positive relationship between returnees and stayers in many ethnically mixed communities (Kleck, 2006).

However, the ongoing complexity of economic and political transformation processes also created new social division and fostered other forms of social differences in such communities. These differences have been seen through the lens of a new, emerging ethnic division of the country involving religious, economic or other individual or structural characteristics embedded in the everyday lives of the population of BiH and within the region.

According to Capo and Halilovich (2013) prewar relationships and networks in a postconflict environment might be interrupted by new minority-majority relationships at the local as well as the national level. This refers not only to different ethnicities but also to different migration experiences such as those of ex-diaspora returnees, IDPs and nonmigrants (Povrzanovic-Frykman, 2003; Stefansson, 2007; Kaya, 2009), with their new emerging social-economic status. For example, a certain level of mistrust and distance has been created between those who fled the country during the war and those who stayed behind (Kaya, 2009). The same difficulties in (re)building social relationships have been noticeable between IDPs, seen as newcomers, and nonmigrants.

The postconflict environment has become a space of potentially new social gaps, following new social orders and social divisions for all three groups considered here. It is therefore important to explore what are common (specific) determinants of social capital among people with different migration experiences – external migrants, internal migrants and nonmigrants – and how relevant they are in regards to ongoing economic, political and social transformation processes. It is essential to consider what links them and what separates them to understand social capital and its features in a postconflict environment.

Social capital and its determinants have been a highly contested field of research. It certainly appears difficult to understand the relationship between individuals, households, communities and associations, on the one hand, and market, state and nongovernmental organizations, on the other, when defining and assessing social capital. Actually, a difficulty in transferring social capital from an individual (understood as social means for personal goals) to an aggregated (the process of socialisation and political discourse) level remains the main obstacle when investigating social capital. This includes both structural and individual levels, including social skills, trust, reciprocity, exchange, obligation, in-group belonging, norms, values systems, ethnicity, religious identity and other socio cultural markers (Bourdieu, 1980, 1986; Coleman, 1988, Lin, 1998; Portes, 1998; Putnam, 2000; Adler and Kwon, 2002; Grossman, 2013). At the same time, this complexity opens up a space for a variety of opportunities to reach different individual and collective goals (Bourdieu, 1986; Coleman, 1988; Lin, 1999; Putnam, 1993, 2000).

A number of studies (Costa and Khan, 2003; Alexander, 2007; Chritoforou, 2011; Mondejar-Jimenez *et al.*, 2011) suggest that, in order to understand the probability of an individual becoming a member of a group or social network – transmitting values, and displaying reciprocity and cooperation – social capital should be investigated through individual determinants such as education, employment, sex, gender, marital status and other similar characteristics. At the same time, group membership is strongly affected by aggregate variables. The importance of systems, country-specific factors influenced by history and culture, welfare system, political environment, ethnic diversity, labour market condition, marriage conventions and gender roles, should not be neglected. Moreover, a need to interlink and consolidate the determinants of social capital at different levels – macro, meso and micro – has been widely confirmed in the literature. In most of the previous studies, the determinants of social capital have been investigated by considering individual and group characteristics and membership within the structural environment (Glaeaser *et al.*, 2002). Very often individual characteristics such as higher income and education lead to higher social capital (Hellermann, 2006). It is also a known fact that those with higher social status are more likely to engage in more social interactions both at the personal level and the structural level. Other studies emphasize the importance of other individual factors such as age, life experiences, qualifications, gender and employment, in the accumulation of social capital. At the same time, these individual attributes influence how individuals access and utilize their political orientation, personal freedom, ethics or religiosity (Christoforou, 2011). Finally, the individual practice of social capital depends considerably on how individual assessments of social obligations reflect norms and values that are shaped and sustained at a more aggregated level (Chrisofornu, 2011).

The determinants of social capital should not, therefore, be perceived through a single set of fixed characteristics; they should rather be investigated as multidimensional in nature – in terms of groups, networks, norms and trust (Grootaert *et al.*, 2004). Moreover, structural and relational resources should be taken into consideration when identifying common determinants of social capital at different levels for different migrant groups.

Against this background, and in line with Grootaert *et al.* (2004), in this research we treat social capital as a multidimensional and multilevel phenomenon that reflects trust, networks and groups and prosocial actions at both individual and collective levels. Within this general framework, our project is designed to explore: (i) *common determinants* of social capital that link the migrant groups considered here, including external migrants (ex-diaspora returnees to BiH and BiH external migrants to Serbia and Croatia), internal migrants (internally displaced persons and permanent "resettlers" within BiH) and nonmigrants ("domiciles" or "old dwellers" in BiH); and (ii) *specific determinants* that distinguish the three groups in focus. Specifically, to capture the multidimensional and multilevel aspects of social capital, this research is designed to explore relational social capital explored through trust (general and institutional trust); structural social capital, explored through networks (size and structures) and associations/groups; and collective actions and prosocial behaviour, explored through outcomes of relational and structural social capital. We also consider collective activities organized in a "crisis" or "disaster" period around the floods in 2014.

The SEE Sample in Focus

The qualitative research sample was designed in accordance with structural and individual characteristics of the SEE region and the migrant groups. To elaborate on the common and specific determinants of social capital in postconflict environments on the ground, the project focused on three different migrant groups: (i)external migraines – ex-diaspora returnees, external BiH migrants to Serbia and Croatia; (ii) internal migrants – internally displaced persons; (iii) nonmigrants. The inclusion of Serbia and Croatia in the project, in addition to BiH, is due to the large presence of BiH migrants in these countries, which therefore provides an insight into the migrants' experiences in a different structural context within the region. The sample is based on 100 interviews: 60 interviews in BiH (20 domiciles/nonmigrants; 20 internal migrants; 20 external migrants), with 20 additional interviews with BiH external migrants in Serbia and 20 in Croatia. In framing our sample, particular attention was given to the role of ethnicity, including all ethnicities in the sampled areas.

The data were collected through fieldwork conducted between April and September 2015 in three SEE countries: BiH, Serbia and Croatia. The fieldwork included a pilot questionnaire, a semistructured questionnaire, participant observation and a number of informal talks with all three of the groups being investigated (Bosnians, Serbians and Croatians). In each country, the interviews were conducted in several locations. The selection of locations was made mainly according to the ethnicities of all three groups, taking into account the majority-minority ethnic ratio between the groups and geographic criteria (urban, semiurban and rural areas). Individual characteristics – including age, education, gender, employment and family status – were taken into consideration for selection of the interviewees.

In most cases, the interviews were arranged in advance by phone or sometimes directly through face-to-face contact. The interviews were conducted both in public and private spaces and lasted from 15 minutes to 1.5 hours. The anonymity of personal data was guaranteed and all the principles of ethical research were strictly followed. In total, 85 interviews were recorded and transcribed verbatim, while 15 interviews involved taking written field notes. The reason for this was that 15 participants preferred not to be voice recorded for personal reasons and difficulty in sharing their personal stories. Most of the unrecorded interviews were collected within the nonmigrant group, with whom extensive ethnographic conversations and participant observation were carried out, along with the fieldwork. In order to respect the anonymity of the personal data, all interviewees were deidentified and coded by their migrant status and location: external migrants (BiH-RB 01-20; Serbia-RS 01-20; Croatia-RC 01-20), internal migrants (Republika Srpska – IDPRS 01-14; FBiH – IDPFBiH 14–20) and nonmigrants (Republika Srpska – NMRS 01-12; FBiH – NMFBiH 12–20). The context of interviews usually included informal chats, followed by formal semistructured interviews, covering the questions and areas prepared for the quantitative part of the research project. The general questions in the quantitative and qualitative part of the research were extended to include more specific questions and subthemes in the qualitative questionnaire. For the qualitative research, the questionnaire was designed to follow the individual stories of each interviewee and their everyday lives and to focus on the important details wherever a need for this was noticed. This approach provided an opportunity to develop further discussion about other important subject(s) and themes for each person/group in focus.

The fieldwork proceeded without major difficulties with exception of the case of BiH external migrants in Croatia and IDPs and nonmigrants of Croat ethnicity in BiH. Certain obstacles in arranging interviews in Croatia as well as with Croat ethnic groups in BiH appeared in the course of research. The majority of the interviews initially arranged were cancelled afterwards. No particular explanations for cancellations were given by any of the contacted individuals. We dealt with such cancellations by recruiting new participants, which required additional time and logistical considerations.

Bosnia and Herzegovina

The fieldwork in BiH was conducted in the period between April and July 2015. In total, 60 people were interviewed in several locations: Banja Luka (25), Gradiška (5), Teslić (8), Šamac (3), Bugojno (3), Goražde (3), Kotor Varoš (1); Jelah (6); Ključ (1); Mostar (3) and Dubica (3). The interviews were organized as follows: 20 external migrants (ex-diaspora returnees to BiH); 20 IDPs (internally displaced people or internal migrants)[4] and 20 nonmigrants ("domicile" population). The interviewed cohort came from all three ethnic groups: Bosniacs (25); Serbs (26) and Croats (9). The selection of interviewees was based mainly on their migrant status (ex-diaspora returnees, IDPs or internal migrants and nonmigrants) and their ethnicity, followed by the majority-minority relationships in selected locations. The individual characteristics of selected interviewees such as age, gender, family status, education and employment were taken into consideration

---

4   In our research we have collected data that cover internally displaced persons who moved mainly because of the war but also data on internally displaced people who moved voluntarily, and mainly for economic reasons after the war, but sometimes even during the war period. We acknowledge that sometimes it is hard to identify which motives prevailed (because they can mix) but when we do have a clear indication regarding the category, we are precise in our conclusions.

in the sampling process. In addition to individual interviews, a number of interviews were carried out within the households and included the main respondents' family members. This approach was used to identify the patterns of social capital within the households as well as the level of (in)equality within the households. The findings showed that the socioeconomic status of the interviewed population in BiH was diverse. For instance, the ex-diaspora returnees mainly engage in small businesses and/ or temporary migration and their housing situation is resolved whereas the internal migrants (or IDPs) are mainly employed in the public/private sector, self-employed or unemployed, frequently with an unresolved housing situation. Similarly, the nonmigrants are mainly employed in public/ private sector or are unemployed, without housing difficulties.

Serbia

The fieldwork in Serbia was conducted in the period between June and August 2015. In total 30 people were interviewed in two locations: Belgrade (16) and Novi Sad (14). All of those interviewed belonged to the Serbian ethnic group. Most of them were resettled in Serbia during the war in BiH, although several emigrated after being IDPs in BiH, or for studying and working reasons in the previous 10 years. All of them had experienced several resettlements during their stay in Serbia. The majority of them first moved into the smaller cities in Serbia, where they had some relatives or friends. Later, within a year or two, they moved to the main centres in Serbia – mostly Belgrade and Novi Sad. They are mainly self-employed or employed in the public or private sectors. All of them have obtained Serbian citizenship and resolved their housing situation through private funding. The majority did not receive any state support for housing and employment.

Croatia

The fieldwork in Croatia was conducted in the period between August and September 2015. In total, 20 people were interviewed in three locations: Zagreb (5), Karlovac (4) and Ogulin (11). The interviewed population belonged to the Croat (15) and Bosniac (5) ethnic groups. They all were resettled in Croatia during the war in BiH, i.e. between 1992 and 1995. The majority were living in the places where they first resettled. All of them obtained Croat citizenship from the period of their arrival, except some Bosniacs. While the Croat population obtained citizenship automatically, for Bosniacs it took several years to complete the same procedure. All of them have resolved their housing situation mainly through state support (*darovnica*) or occasionally through private funding. The state has also provided support in the labour market and included BiH external migrants in various employment programs. However, those programs have been in low-income or insecure jobs. Consequently, many of the interviewed participants were taking part in the social security program in Croatia and they were provided with social and health benefits by the state.

Discussion of the Results based on Interviews

Trust (General and Specific)

With a relative decline of formal hierarchies and difficulties in political-economic transformation processes, the development of flexible social arrangements is becoming an indispensable part of everyday life in all three countries: BiH, Serbia and Croatia. These arrangements are built upon trust among the people through their everyday interactions, either on a personal level or at institutional levels. Trust is therefore an essential feature of social capital and an integral part of each of its dimensions, and as a relational domain of attitudes of people it might be approached as both general and specific (Grootaert *et al.*, 2014).

In our research, the question of trust was understood as people's general confidence in other people and institutions as well as specific trust in individuals, groups and institutions (Rebmann *et al.*, 2017). Consequently, we asked the respondents to reflect on their general trust in (unknown) people and institutions (service providers) at the state and entity levels, followed by more specific trust in certain individuals and institutions at the local levels.

We find that general trust in people and institutions across all three countries (BiH, Serbia and Croatia) is rather low. For all groups examined, general trust in institutions and people weakened over time. The interviewees stressed that general mistrust in both people and institutions emerged through a lack of political and economic transformation over the past 20 years, which has strongly influenced the attitudes of people. Many of these opinions were connected to their migrant experiences and personal sociocultural characteristics (such as education, ethnicity, religious and class) and socioeconomic status (such as employment, housing and social security).

Generalized Trust

In BiH, all three categories of people who were examined – external migrants, internal migrants and nonmigrants –expressed a lack of general trust in people and institutions. The majority agreed that today it is necessary to be careful with people, while the institutional environment at the state level (and entity levels in BiH) is perceived as inadequate. This indicates that institutional efficiency might not be as expected by general people, which might cause a negative effect on the economic environment in the end (e.g. Efendic and Pugh, 2015). For external migrants in BiH, most of these opinions were based on personal experiences after their return to BiH. The external BiH migrants considered that social relations between people have been weakening over time due to a lack of political-economic transformation processes and a complicated institutional environment. According to a 54-year-old female (entrepreneur) returnee in BiH, the situation in BiH is far from what she had expected it to be upon her return. She perceives the institutional environment as very complicated and highly corrupt. She believes that

> ... in general, people can't be trusted ... [it] depends from case to case how this is visible, but it seems that here all has been changed and people look for material benefits by any means: cheating, being corrupt, stealing ... all. But I'm not surprised that nothing is functioning here. There is no efficient state, you can't trust any politician while the bureaucracy here is a nightmare. Ever since I returned I'm struggling with the administration and bureaucracy. All jobs seem to be done "under the table". I remember during the Yugoslav times, it wasn't like that. As well in Norway, where I spent last 20 years. I also can notice how much all segments of the society have changed.

Similar stories reflecting frustration with the "system" and lack of trust have been recorded among internal migrants and nonmigrants in BiH. In the case of internal migrants, a lack of trust has been particularly linked to their status as IDPs and a lack of institutional support for their settlement and integration in the host communities. This primarily refers to employment, social security and housing as well as an often unfriendly and hostile reception in the host communities. A 50-year-old female internal migrant in BiH-RS sees her struggles for integration in 1990s as an endless process. She came to Banja Luka from Mostar at the beginning of the 1990s and she still lives in rented accommodation without formal employment:

> As IDPs we couldn't resolve our housing, after all these years I still haven't resolved the situation with my flat in Mostar, and I asked all relevant institutions to help. Down [she refers to FBiH] don't want to hear this story; here [in Republika Srpska (RS)] none takes care and so on. At the end, I still pay rent, I have to go to private medical. I simply don't trust anyone and anything here. We came here from Mostar because my husband is a Serb and I'm a Croat. He was also a pilot in the military but then he got a health problem. And all people and institutions turned their back on us ["okrenuli su nam leđa"]. Even our friends! Now, I'm managing through some part-time jobs in the service sector … but I honestly lost any hope for anything [better] here.

Similarly, other internal migrants report a lack of general trust in people and institutions through the lens of minority-majority relationships. Today most cities in BiH are likely to be highly "ethnicized", with one ethnic group representing a majority and others minorities. According to a 55-year-old male internal migrant, this still poses a significant problem to many people. The political struggles around the country and monopoly on political power by the ethnonationalistic political elites continue to affect everyday lives of ordinary people across the country. As one of our respondents expressed it:

> I don't trust any institution in this country. Just look at my municipality – two or three families are ruling the city. This has been so for years and years. Nothing to be done against that when you see that the whole country is like that. I am still paying a rent here. We [his wife and him] just work to maintain living costs and afford education to our children. All society is still divided between Bosniacs and Croats, even in kindergartens! I just don't see myself as a part of this society and I try to keep myself apart [from it]. My family and only a few friends, that's my life here.

Nonmigrants also feel a lack of general trust in people and institutions. They feel that everyday life has become too politicized and corrupt. For a 50-year-old couple in RS, who have been mainly involved in informal employment, nostalgia for the old times is important as they reflect on the current political and economic situation:

> Unfortunately, we have now become an environment where you have to be careful with people and you can't trust the institutions at all!! We are simply part of one global disorder, which came after one solid system we enjoyed before. All are corrupted now and people's behaviour is just about that. As an ethnic member of one group you can't simply trust or rely on them! All of them are thieves ["pljačkaši"] and all are corrupted, at all three institutional levels.

We found a slight difference in the perception of trust among those with higher education and better employment status. According to a 40-year-old internal migrant employed in the RS government, careful behaviour with people is necessary but the institutional environment needs better understanding among the people:

> In general, it's necessary to be careful with the people, and for the institutions I think that the least trust exists at the state level because of the system we have but also because people don't know who are the people that we voted for and what they should represent at the state level. I think that here is still present the trend of the cult of personality [*kult ličnosti*] when politics and trust come into question. I think that there's a lack of interest in engaging ourselves in issues at the higher institutional level is very present in these spaces.

Similar opinions were expressed by nonmigrants in BiH. The majority of interviews conducted with nonmigrants can be summarized in a quote from a 54-year-old local official in FBiH, who claims that the situation in BiH has worsened over time:

> I don't trust people anymore. Back two-three years before, I did but now I don't trust anyone. Everything is too much politicized. [...] You need "private connections" [*veze*] in any place you go. The job search is exclusively connected to the politics and it's not important what you know, but who you know. The power of politics is in everything: in employment, health, culture, in all – at least I think like that.

The situation in Serbia and Croatia has been rather similar to that in BiH. The stories recorded in Serbia and Croatia also indicate a lack of general trust in people and institutions. For many, a lack of general trust in people and institutions is linked to their migrant status and a lack of state support in resolving their socioeconomic difficulties. This includes employment and housing as well as struggles to integrate into society with the nonmigrant population in host communities. For example, upon their arrival in Serbia, a majority of the BiH external migrants claimed that they had been left on their own. Although they were granted Serbian citizenship without difficulty, a lack of state support when they arrived put them in a difficult situation. They did not receive any support for their integration in the labour market or to solve their housing problems. That has been frequently followed by a certain mistrust of the domicile population towards BiH external migrants. Their opinions might be summarized by a quote of a 45-year-old female medical doctor, who has been living with her family in Serbia since 1994:

> I don't have almost any trust in institutions here. All the time we see the same people and I don't have trust in any political party here. Before I did, but I lost every hope. I feel in a way equal to the population here to vote and be politically engaged but I'm sure that in their eyes that's quite different. This is not an easy society and people are very closed. Just as an example, in my previous job I was usually accused of helping only people from Bosnia and the same was coming when we were resolving our housing problem. We bought a car and an apartment, all of that on credit!! In the eyes of other people this became a big question as "you are refugee", where do you get the money … and they made a lot of difficulties for us. At the end, we left that place and moved to another city. So, how and whom to trust?

In Croatia, the situation has been similar. People frequently expressed a lower level of trust in state institutions and in people in general. However, did not feel isolated in regard to their migrant status or lack of care for them by the state. They all received assistance from the state upon their arrival in Croatia. They were offered help for their housing and employment through several programs. Housing and employment were mostly resolved through donations and subsidies (*darovnica*) and some employment programs offered by the National Agency for Employment. According to a 47-year-old female BiH external migrant in Croatia, despite the generally good environment in Croatia, their migrant experience and position in a new country still creates a lack of general trust in people and institutions:

> In general you have to be careful with people. All our experience here taught us that no one can be trusted completely today. All people think if we are Croats, and we came to Croatia, we are the same. But it's not like that. We came here 20 years ago and we haven't been treated in the same way as people who have been living here all their lives […] Well, I think that we are so far away from the state institutions. So, I don't trust them so much, as we can't actually reach them easily. I feel that we still

can't have our voice at the state level. It's just good that we managed to get the houses, and some jobs [...] Still, most of these jobs are just those at very low level, what the "domicile population" is not willing to do.

From the interviews conducted with all three of the groups across three countries – BiH, Serbia and Croatia – it might be concluded that general trust in people and institutions was very weak. Although certain distinctions between these three groups exist, it might be possible to draw some general conclusions. For all the three groups, socioeconomic status, migrant experience and their personal characteristics play an important role in their answers about general trust in people and institutions. A majority agrees that today it is necessary to be very careful with people while the institutional environment at the state level is perceived as inadequate. For example, the external migrants in BiH perceive that the institutional environment in BiH is very complicated and corrupt and this opinion is frequently shared with both internal migrants and nonmigrants. All of them further acknowledge that lack of trust in institutions also reflects the lack of trust among people. However, the internal migrants still regard their migrant status, the ethnic division of the country and personal characteristics as the main reasons for a lack of general trust in people and institutions in BiH. The lack of state support for employment, housing and social security, and an unfriendly, hostile reception, as well as the minority-majority relationship became important for their everyday lives. At the same time, those with better education and employment status maintain slightly greater trust in institutions but not in people. The situation is similar in Serbia and Croatia, where the majority of BiH external migrants live. In Serbia, for example, the BiH external migrants see a lack of general trust in institutions and people in a lack of state support in resolving their problems with employment and housing. Many interviewees described their struggles to integrate into the "domicile population" in Serbia as equally important. In Croatia, the situation has been very similar. However, the low trust in institutions has not been followed by the low trust in the population. People consider that they have been rather well accepted by the host society, while the instuitional environment has not been favourable despite several programmes offered by the state in order to resolve their housing and employment issues.

Specific Trust

A general lack of trust in people and institutions among all three groups and countries has been largely replaced by trust in specific individuals and groups of people as well as institutions. That specific trust for all three categories has been built up around their lives at local level and around local institutions. This also includes several more elements such as their personal characteristics (education, ethnicity, class) and their migration experiences.

In BiH, all three categories of migrants are very much attached to their municipalities in terms of both people and institutions. Their trust is mostly directed to their families and close friends, while local institutions might compensate for the lack of trust in the institutions at higher administrative levels, although this is rare. For example, the external migrants frequently speak of their return to their families and their feelings of belonging to a specific local place. They also often mention a certain level of trust in the local institutions, although this is at a very low level. For instance, for a 51-year-old female returnee, her return to FBiH, her everyday life, is organized around her family and some close friends, including some engagement with and trust in the local institutions. However, she still sees importance of relationships in her city that were disrupted due to the ethnic division of population and people's self-interest:

> I'm still managing, all thanks to family and trust in certain people ... that is how I'm finding my jobs and helping my family. Sometimes [...] bad experiences happen. But I still keep faith in certain people, and people in positions. That is only at the local level and people who are not looking at nationality, ethnic belonging, people who simply want to help. Since my return I've been struggling to resolve my status the best I could and I was also engaging in political activities, as a representative of a minority group in my city, but after the elections, it is always the same story: they use us to help them in local elections, but afterwards, no promises are kept. With exception of some people! So, I rather trust only certain local public officials but not the local institutions in general.

Similar stories were found among internal migrants, who stressed that their everyday life is organized around their trust in family and close friends. Most of these close relationships were shared with people who had the same migration experiences and who were from the same place of origin. That, however, might be different from place to place and might depend on people's personal characteristics such as their education, ethnicity, class and location (urban, semiurban or rural areas). This, again, can be tied to their trust in the local institutions, which is slightly higher than trust in the institutions at the state and entity level. According to a 57-year-old internal migrant couple in RS, who live in a semiurban area, some people in their neighbourhood could still be trusted regardless of their migrant status, although the same could not be said for local institutions:

> We first came here because we had our relatives. Then we gathered with some people who were also internally displaced as we did and we started to look for the work together. We were working on farms or anywhere where it was paid. Now we live among "domiciles" here and they treat as quite well. They are helping a lot, for temporary jobs, information, similar stuff, but still most of the social interactions are with people who were internally displaced, as we were. It's a different place; here neighbours don't go to their neighbour for daily coffees and other things. But, if you ask them [referring to nonmigrants] they will help. So, I do still have a certain trust in some people here. The biggest disappointments are the local authorities. They didn't do anything for us. So we don't trust any [of them] here.

At the same time, for those internal migrants settled in urban areas, specific trust is still limited to a certain number of people. Most of them share specific trust with certain people with the same migration experience and education level, while ethnicity is rather neglected. Many actually feel unaccepted by nonmigrants and people with different socioeconomic status. A 51-year-old male internal migrant in a city in RS, states that specific trust is still more related to migration status and education rather than ethnic belonging:

> The centre of my life is my family and two friends. I trust only them. They share the same suffering as I do. So, we usually share our stories and try to help each other as much as possible. Life for us is still hard here … We are still considered to be refugees, and second-class citizens [*građani drugog reda*]. I'm not saying that you can't trust anyone because of that, but in my neighbourhood we are surrounded by "domicile population". I have to admit that until today we didn't manage to have any communication with them. They are not rejecting us but they do blame us for all their problems. As we came and took over their city, their jobs, their "culture", all. And, at work, I'm still just a low-level worker, as I have only secondary school and do some physical jobs.

A certain level of disruption in the relationships between people with different migration experiences was suggested by interviews with the non-migrant population. The core of their specific trust and everyday lives are still families and close friends, while everyday life is greatly influenced by nostalgia for the prewar times and social life. Many claimed that the "newcomers" influenced many social transformations taking a place in the cities around BiH. As was stated by a 44-year-old female nonmigrant in RS, who indirectly sees the situation in her city through the lens of the new social orders emerging through the new "refugee" population, who "inhabit" the city today:

> Well, I still trust just certain people here. That is maybe two-three persons, who I've known whole my life. I'm not saying that people who live now here threaten our positions. In some of them I see new friends who replaced those who left. But, I'm not identifying them with the old ones. I haven't noticed any problem at my work place. But on the street, yes. I do! Our old culture of the place is totally lost. All good norms are put aside, and I have to admit that this bothers me a lot.

With regard to specific forms of trust, similar stories were recorded in Serbia and Croatia. Migrant experiences and strong feelings of belonging to a place of origin in BiH are essential for BiH external migrants in Serbia and Croatia to build trusting relationships, apart from those with family and close friends. Ethnicity and religious affiliation also played an important role in forming those relationships. For example, according to a 46-year-old male BiH external migrant in Serbia, his social activities are organized mainly around family and trust in people originating from BiH. The role of ethnicity and religion should not be neglected in this process as well:

> I feel nice here [Novi Sad], but generally I prefer to trust mainly people from Bosnia. Around 90% of my friends are actually from Bosnia. I think that we are different. People here are more attached to each other and also they can't put themselves in our position [he refers to the war experience and migration]. I always keep my life with people across Drina. Well, from recently as well with those of my religion. Before, as all of us in former Yugoslavia, I didn't have any connection to religion, but after the war and my migrant experience, religion has become important to me and I've started to practise it more. So, that became important and I trust more people who share the same feeling about my religion.

We observed similar trends in Croatia. Besides trusting people with the same migrant experiences and shared feelings of belonging to a certain place in BiH, there is noticeable trust in local institutions. Moreover, many BiH external migrants in Croatia have been very active in political life at the local level and they see their municipalities as very effective; as a 47-year-old male BiH external migrant stated:

> I trust most local institutions here. I mean, I have been satisfied until now [...], nothing is perfect, but if you ask for something they will help you if they can. That's why I'm also engaged in politics here. Actually, we are divided here between those who are right and left oriented. To be honest, for example, I had a friend from my city in Bosnia, who I've known all my life, but he votes right wing and I prefer left political options, so we don't communicate anymore. But, apart of this experience, I still trust people from BiH. We still share the same way of thinking, jokes and we all long for Bosnia very much.

The lack of general trust in institutions and people for all three groups and across all three countries has been largely replaced with the specific forms of trust. Specific trust is understood as trust in specific people, networks and institutions, mostly at the local level. It is noticeable by all three groups and in all three countries. That trust is based on specific individual-cultural characteristics as well as migration experiences and socioeconomic status. For example, the BiH external migrants' lack of general trust has been compensated for by trust in family and close friends relationships at the local level and their migrant experiences. This is often accompanied by a higher level of trust in local institutions. However, these relationships are still strongly influenced by personal characteristics such as education, class, ethnicity or local belonging. Internal migrants in BiH express the same opinion about general and specific trust. Moreover, those with higher education and better jobs frequently have more trust in people in their local municipalities regardless of their migration experiences. They consider education as a core of trust and communication. The nonmigrants in BiH maintain specific trust within their families and for close friends, who are most likely also a part of their prewar relationships. Among all three groups, their specific trust was built on their feelings of the isolation in comparison to other nonmigrant groups. At the same time, in Serbia and Croatia, the BiH external migrants expressed specific trust in certain people and institutions. Besides family, their trust has been invested in people with the same migration experiences and from the same place of origin. Moreover, ethnicity and religious affiliation appeared as important features of specific trust. This is fostered by the fact that religious and ethnic aspirations emerged out of their migration experiences. In Croatia, specific trust in local institutions has been linked to migrants' engagement in politics at the local level. Many of BiH external migrants in Croatia have been politically active and their trust in institutions has been linked to a political party with which they are associated.

Networks and Groups/Associations as Dimensions of Social Capital

Due to a lack of common trust and increase in specific forms of trust, as described above, a variety of informal networks emerged in all three categories and countries: BiH, Serbia and Croatia. As the presence of trust in a social structure or society, as well as social norms, might be considered as essential for social capital to emerge (Coleman, 1988), these networks are likely to play a crucial role in the everyday lives of our respondents. In particular, the BiH external migrants in all three countries and BiH internal migrants have been managing their economic and social problems mainly through these "migrant networks". However, as Grootaert *et al.* (2004) argue, identifying a common feature of a network, its size and internal diversity, remains the main difficulty in defining the network. The networks are frequently related to personal characteristics and they might exist separately from other forms of formal groups and associations. People can become involved in various informal networks based on their daily interactions (Putnam, 1993, 2000). This interaction might vary from a variety of informal chats, established between those with similar demographic characteristics, such as neighbourhoods, ethnicity, religion, education, work, class and so on, to memberships in more formal groups and associations. In order to build a certain form of social capital out of these interactions, a person usually needs time and effort to build and gain trust developed among people, also including obligations and expectations. This depends on trustworthiness of the social environment, the information-flow capability of the social structure (Coleman, 1988) and access to networks (Tzanakis, 2013).

In our research, networks were approached through people's everyday communication, interaction and expectations as well as through obligations and norms within wider society and at the workplace. In addition to these forms of networking, the research participants were also asked to share their opinion and experiences of participation in groups and associations. The conducted interviews indicate that family, migrant status, education, ethnicity, religion and class still play an important role in everyday interactions for all three categories. To a certain extent, there is a noticeable level of intersection between these elements, while in many cases they are still very much based on some specific personal characteristics and specific migration experiences. Moreover, with regard to specific trust, the majority shared their daily communication with their families and close friends with similar socioeconomic and migrant status, both within their neighbourhoods and at their workplaces. The issues discussed in these communications usually started with personal matters, including economic issues and political and other social themes. A majority of the respondents reported certain expectations as well as obligations that are particularly oriented towards family and close friends. At the same time, negative opinions and lower level of participation in the groups and associations were influenced by a lack of general trust in institutions and people in all three countries, followed by emerging power relations within the groups and general view of the purpose of the membership. The main findings are elaborated further below.

In BiH, the networks for all three categories depend mainly on their personal characteristics, their migrant experiences and the locality (neighbourhoods/rural-urban areas). For all three groups, family remains the core of organizing their everyday social life as well as engaging in certain networks. For example, external and internal migrants in BiH frequently indicate that they had an "easier communication" with those with similar migrant status and shared integration difficulties. At the same time, they stress the importance of some personal characteristics (such as education and ethnicity) and socioeconomic status (such as employment, housing and social security). Generally speaking, over time, for a majority of respondents, these networks have become weaker. According to the results from interviews, the main reason seems to be related to the difficulties associated with the ongoing political and economic transition processes, which reflects a lack of general trust in people and institutions in BiH.

In addition, many external migrants still felt very negatively influenced by the ethnic division of the country and the majority-minority categorization there. According to a 50-year-old external migrant in FBiH, communication in his city proceeds without difficulties but many tensions still exist between the two dominant ethnic groups. A 52-year-old male external migrant in FBiH stated that networks in his city are still very much influenced by ethnicity and family and sustained by everyday interactions within a divided society:

> The communication within the neighbourhood is general good. But, still, all depends on what you bring from home. I get scared when I hear young people talking about other ethnicities so badly. This must be coming from their homes; from where else? But also when you think that in our city the schools and even kindergartens, are divided between Bosniacs and Croats, you are not surprised. I have a good relationship

> here with all people. We are now sitting in a Serbian restaurant and I'm probably one of the rare people who is coming here. To be honest, I'm also keeping myself calm. I communicate with my family and a few friends. For the rest I don't have a time and I think it's better even not to engage. We live in strange times and you never know what to expect from the other side. But, still, I'm managing all thanks to good people and friends. I have found my job thanks to a friend's recommendation, who is Croat. And if I need anything, I will first go to my sister and family.

At the same time, internal migrants consider that, beside ethnicity, their migrant status and the difficulty integrating into a new society are still important aspects of their daily communication and interactions with society. For the majority, these networks have played an important role in resolving their issues around jobs and housing. Many actually managed to find jobs through these networks and built up their houses by supporting other internal migrants. This is a characteristic of semiurban and rural areas in particular. In an interview with two internal migrant women (IDPs) who had become close friends upon their arrival in a city in RS, the same ordeal brought them together. This was strengthened by their shared feeling of isolation and alienation from the community in which they settled:

> I came here because I have family here. It was hard at the beginning. We (IDPs) were all settled in one area in the former Muslim houses. After a while, we had to move and now I am renting a house. I still couldn't manage to resolve my housing but I was lucky to get a job. I've started with the lowest paid job, as a cleaner and later I managed to improve my position thanks to some private contacts and support of my family members. In general, I don't communicate with a lot of people. Only with my family and a few friends! I also don't make any division between people, but most of my friends are also people who came here during the war. I can't say that I face some difficulties because of my status. People are in general kind, although there is no deeper communication neither in my neighbourhood nor in the city, the same holds for my workplace. But, still, there is a lot of division there, especially you are forced to communicate with people who treat you as "a third-class person".

Furthermore, according to her friend, a 49-year-old female internal migrant (IDP), class, education and social status are also considered as important features of their daily lives:

> Yes, it was important who came and how someone managed herself/himself. Those with higher education got better jobs, resolve most of their problems. I had big expectations from them, as they are people who share the same experience. I felt this particularly when I started to search for jobs for my sons … when I went to ask for

help, I just received a negative answer. So, I rely mostly on a few good friends, with the same experiences, education and job position. One of them is IDPs, as I am and another is not. But, it's still very hard to feel this place as "home". I have a feeling that even today all is divided between domicile [*domaći*] and refugees [*izbjeglice*]. But, at the end, if you don't have a good position or money you are nothing. No one actually cares for you.

Good relationships among internal migrants, especially those living in common neighbourhoods, were important in resolving various socioeconomic challenges, such as housing problems. Many built their houses through join action and help each other. As a 60-year-old male IDP in a city in RS reported:

In the neighbourhood where I live, we are all IDPs. We have very good relationships among each other. We built our houses thanks to joint actions. You know, it was hard to find your own shelter when you don't have anything, so usually after you find a job, usually as a labourer, you can get a loan from the bank and start to think about building a house for your family and we actually do that by helping each other. We were organizing "working actions" and we all joined our forces to help and we still keep helping each other. But, when it comes to local institutions [*mjesne zajednice*] then you see the difference between us [IDPs] and the domicile population. Our voice is hardly heard and most of the time our demands/inquiries are neglected by domiciles, so our networks are the core of our lives.

At the same time, some other internal migrants indicated that the relationships between the internal migrants in their neighbourhoods are rather problematic. According to a 57-year-old female internal migrant in RS, although her neighbourhood is inhabited only by internal migrants, various difficulties are still present in her everyday life:

We all here share the same experiences, we had to leave our homes and we all have been going through various struggles to settle down. But I feel all the time just their envy and hate. People just look what you have and then gossip. They are looking just for problems in your house so they can talk about that and what is worse is that they would rather go to buy from a stranger than from you. I mean, we are all struggling to do some private informal businesses, because we couldn't find formal employment. And you hope that your neighbour will come to buy something from you and help you, so we can all at least survive. But, that has not been happening. I don't know what is in these people; were they all like that always or this economic situation make them like that? I personally prefer to stay only in family circles and not to communicate with others around.

In a similar way, the nonmigrants usually see difficulties in networking and daily communication due to a profound change of the local population in recent decades. In the interviews, they frequently complain that "new-comers" (referring to IDPs and other population from the same entity who came after the war) have disrupted their societies and have largely pushed them to the margins. Moreover, they see that strong networks between the "newcomers" (mostly IDPs and migrants from other parts of BiH) have created various difficulties for their integration into the labour market and have established a new local "culture". Nonmigrants, often see themselves as "others" or "strangers" in their "own cities". They have consequently been building their everyday lives within their small neighbourhoods and with a very close circle of prewar friendships, as the comments of a 41-year-old male in a city in RS show:

> I can't recognize this place anymore; all these people came here and settled them-selves, they seem to be so well connected and you just see how they look after each other. Actually, if you are not from Glamoč or Mrkonjić Grad you don't exist here in Banja Luka. They own the city now!! It's so embarrassing, to be honest. I was born here, raised, and I can't even get the most simple job done. But if I'm one of them, I know that all will be resolved for me. I can't stand them really!! They distorted all good in this place. This palace was so urban and look at it now! It is worse than a village! They don't know even how to behave in the city. I actually don't move any-more from my neighbourhood, where still some of my old friends live. We stay in very close circles and try to prevent ourselves from all this primitivism [*seljakluk*]. I still keep all my relationships also with those who are urban people [*urbana raja*].

However, even for nonmigrants, it is important to acknowledge that in their daily communication and interaction, personal characteristics, such as class and employment, still play an important role. For those with better jobs, the changes in their areas are noticeable but still not necessarily in their daily communication and interaction within society. According to a 55-year-old male entrepreneur in a city of FBiH, the newly arrived popu-lation in his city did not have a strong influence on his social life and he even considers them "useful":

> Well, I communicate with a lot of people because of my business. I don't like politics but I have to engage because of my business, and I don't pay attention who is who, from where and so on. I just know what I have to do for my business to keep it run-ning, and the rest of my free time I daily spend with my friends from a childhood. I simply separate work form my private communication. But I think both are important

because I manage also to do a lot for my friends and family through my interaction with people on positions.

For BiH external migrants in Serbia and Croatia, in addition to their migrant status, their feelings of belonging to a place in BiH has been at the core of their networks. Regardless of their integration into the new society, they have still been organizing their everyday lives around and with people from the same place of origin. These networks played an important role in resolving their employment and housing issues, as was the case for internal migrants in BiH. This has been partly influenced by a lack of state-sponsored social integration of BiH migrants in Serbia as well as a lack of integration into the new society. Despite a lack of state programs to support BiH external migrants in Serbia, many Bosnians see themselves different from the domestic population in Serbia. According to a 50-year-old couple, who are currently employed as sellers at a market place, people from BiH are much closer to each other than to the nonmigrant population. They have been relying on each other in their everyday lives for important issues for a long time:

> In our neighbourhood all houses are owned by the people from Bosnia. We are the same. People here are nice but they are not like us [Bosnians]. We are simply "different". We communicate with each other, although now a little bit less than before because the work takes lot of time. But, still, we relay a lot on each other. I found all my previous works through my people from Bosnia. We build up our houses by supporting each other. If you need anything we firstly go to someone from Bosnia. Sometimes some tensions also among us appeared but we still rely on each other and we are all still very much related to our homes in Bosnia. That always keeps us close. We go there whenever we can and maybe we would need to think to go back there but children have grown up here and they have built up their lives here, but for us, "home" is always there and not here.

For those with higher education, beside their migrant experiences and nostalgia for BiH, their education and employment status is still a strong point in their social relationships. As a 55-year-old female dentist who has been living in Serbia since the early 1990s stated:

> We have a lot of friends here, but still our best friends are one from our hometown in Bosnia. Most of them studied with us [him and his wife], we are meeting regularly, talking about old days back there, the great times we had, but also we are relying on each other a lot! My husband, who is an engineer, has had a lot of difficulty finding a job, so most of the time he is engaged in some works with one of these friends, and we prefer to stay in these small circles.

In Croatia, the situation has been similar to Serbia. A majority of BiH external migrants still maintain daily interaction among themselves as a core of their social life. This is particularly noticeable for those living in smaller cities and towns. They are in daily communication with each other and they also rely on their networks for urgent matters, including searching for jobs. The following statement made by a 46-year-old male BiH external migrant, who lived in a small city in Croatia since the war, is a good example:

> We really don't have any problems here. All neighbours are correct and nice to us. If I need something urgently, I can rely on any neighbour here. Just we like spending time with people from Bosnia. We have our usual coffees and jokes. Yes, we keep our communication very closely. For many of us these contacts were important to find a job. I was firstly working at one bar owned by a man from Bosnia, then my second job was at the market, where my employer was also from Bosnia, and now I'm working for more than 10 years for one Bosnian family, as a housemaid. And, we all keep very strong ties to our homes in Bosnia although I think that no one thinks about returning there. We find ourselves here.

The findings described above clearly indicate that, among the three groups, across all three countries, there was a general lack of trust in institutions. Our respondents preferred to sustain and build specific forms of trust within informal networks, with which they felt familiar. Often, the informal networks were based on family, migration experiences, socioeconomic status and local belonging as well as individual sociocultural characteristics such as education, ethnicity, religion and class. However, while the intersection of these elements has been noticeable in all interviews, a lot of daily communication is still linked to one of these characteristics and locality (for example, neighbourhood/rural-urban). For example, for the BiH external migrants, the informal networks have been strongly influenced by a minority-majority categorization of the population at the local level. Hence, in predominantly ethnically divided societies, family is the first point of contact for all matters, followed by the people with the same or similar migration experiences or prewar connections. A similar pattern has been observed among the internal migrants in BiH. Their migrant status, ethnicity and the difficulty of integration fostered their internal solidarity and support for each other. This includes their access to, and integration into, the labour market, housing and various other structural features. For example, in neighbourhoods inhabited mainly by the internal migrants (IDPs), their networks remain central for organizing various activities, including collective action to build houses and other communal infrastructure. Moreover, these networks become very important in regards to a lack of communication with and segregation from the nonmigrant population. According to many internal migrants, despite their effort to participate in the public life of their municipality, the nonmigrant population still prevailed and therefore their informal networks have remained at the core of their daily social interactions and their economic and political lives in BiH. In comparison to ethnicity, a majority from all three groups still sees the importance of education and class in the establishment of the informal networks. For the external migrants in Serbia and Croatia informal networks are also crucial in their everyday lives. Besides organizing their lives around the people with the same migration experience, they also referred to these networks as a means for resolving their employment and housing as well as other socioeconomic issues. For example, as was the case of internal migrants in BiH, external migrants in Serbia have built their houses with help from within their own group and neighbourhood. In Croatia, informal networks have been also important in daily social interactions and urgent matters among external migrants.

Formal Groups/Associations

In comparison to informal networking in all three countries, a majority of those interviewed were not members of any formal group or association. The slight differences are acknowledged by external and internal migrants in BiH, as well as in Croatia, who have had some experiences in the groups and associations in BiH. In general, rather negative opinions about groups and associations are very much linked to a lack of general trust in people and institutions. The majority have never been engaged in any formal association/groups but, for those who have some experience with them, various difficulties in organizing and managing power relations are seen as the main problem.

In BiH, external and internal migrants have been most active in different kinds of groups and associations. However, although groups and associations preserve networking based on common goals, such as various political, religious, gender, environmental and other objectives, many external and internal migrants in BiH experienced their membership primarily in the context of their migrant status. According to a 46-year-old female external migrant in RS, her membership in several associations, with different interests including gender and politics, was based mainly on her migrant status and the needs of her family. She sees those engagements as more obligatory than voluntary:

> I'm a member of several organizations because I think it's important as it has been important to me to realize some of my rights as returnee and also help to my family. I would not be able to renovate my home if I hadn't been a member of one association. This association, actually, supported the renovation of more than 50 houses. Also, I got big support from one association to start with the production of blueberry. As an individual, you simply can do anything. If you knock on someone's door and ask as an individual for something you are immediately "suspicious". But, if you are a member of a group its different. I think that all people who returned are much more active in this association not on voluntary base but rather by force. They simply push you to register as returnees or IDPs, which already excludes you from the society. In general, I see these associations as something good, although in this country they are too easily established. So, officially, we have a hundreds of associations but none of them functions on the ground.

Similar cases have been registered among BiH internal migrants, who have also been looking to protect some of their rights through various groups and associations. In general, they see those groups and associations in terms of their potential to support them in the labour market and in society. However, the issue of power relations inside a group and its eventual politicization presents the main problem. In some other examples of internal migrant associations with the same goal – gender and integration in society – difficulties inside the groups prevented them from improving their lives and achieving a common goal. Even if all the members belonged to the same ethnic group, power relations and mistrust in these organizations created a lot of difficulties in their work. A 55-year-old female internal migrant in the RS explained how difficulties in an organization arose from internal problems:

> We established this organization to help each other, to find a space for us [women], to go out of the home and have some common activities. We are all Bosniacs here, but the goal wasn't to create an ethnic organization, but just to help each other to integrate here. However, at the beginning the work was going very well and I still believe that lot of things might be achieved through these organizations. But, if you don't look at your personal interest, but more at your community. You can have one paper just for yourself and other for me. It doesn't work like that. If we want that organization works properly we need to be very honest. Unfortunately, this wasn't our case and we closed the organization in a very bad way and with lot of tensions between us.

Other internal migrants in BiH encountered similar difficulties in the functioning of groups and associations. A 60-year-old male leader of a Serbian association for internal migrants (IDPs) presented the work of his association as very successful. However, his words indicate that his engagement was highly politicized and probably even characterized by nepotism:

> We are an NGO and we are active in 37 municipalities all over RS. Actually, we act as the main organization for protecting the rights of internally displaced people in RS. We have today more than 35,000 members, mostly of Serbian ethnicity, but also others. The profiles are very diverse in terms of education and others characteristics. Our common target is to live normally where we are and to finally overcome that division on IDPs [*izbjeglice*] and domicile population as we are usually accused for coming here and taking all from them. But, we are not guilty that they are sitting here for 60 years without achieving anything! We have very good communication inside the organization and everything works so good although some tensions are always present. I was, for example, accused of helping my family through this organization. I used some connections to find them jobs and also to resolve their housing problems but that damaged the reputation of our organization. I helped also to many people for various issues and, yes, I still only believe in our president of the Republika Srpska and his political party.

At the same time, some internal migrants shared very positive experiences with hometown/regional associations. They saw them as important for their integration in a new society. A 38-year-old female internal migrant in RS considered that a lot of problems and needs could be addressed through these organizations:

> I've been a member of various professional organizations, and I'm also a member of a hometown association. In all cases I consider a membership in any association as advantage, because you are for sure stronger as a group than as an individual. If you are a member of team, your word might count in the society. Because, all groups are gathered together because of some common interests. I personally always felt more superior in these associations and groups. That is especially the case for hometown groups. I think that membership in that organization might be helpful to people to find a job or resolve any other problem. Whenever you come to some new places you feel yourself as "newcomer" [*pridošlica*] and that you have to put much more effort and energy to achieve what others there already have. I strongly believe that everyone would find a way to help to a person from their hometown [*nadje načina da pomogne "svome"*].

In comparison to external and internal migrants in BiH, nonmigrants are rarely active in formal groups and associations. The frequent exclusion from their social life in their hometowns strongly influences their participation in formal groups and associations. The differences are only noticeable in the case of humanitarian actions. The overall opinions of nonmigrants about this issue might be summarized in a quote from two sisters, in their 50s, interviewed in a city in FBiH:

> No, we are not members of any organization. Before the war we were attending different groups such as theatres, choirs, social youth movements and all the nice things we had in the previous time. Afterwards, participation in any group and organization became so pathetic and we are not members anymore. We are not interested; just when there are some humanitarian actions we join our forces with other people. Not long ago we have an example of one small child, who needed a help for her medical treatment. All people helped!! Religious differences, ethnicity, education didn't matter, but these are just occasionally situations.

The membership of BiH external migrants in groups and associations in Serbia and Croatia has been lower than expected. This might have been influenced by the fact that informal networks are well established and functional among these people but also by the fact that formal organizing has failed due to a lack of state support. In Serbia, for example, almost no one has been active in any organization as all their social life has been organized around people from BiH. However, certain initiatives have started to emerge but they are mostly related to political goals, as a 46-year-old BiH external migrant in Serbia observed:

> I don't know that much about this organization since no one has contacted us about that and as I also know, there is no any organization for us with an exception that recently one organization, named Dinara-Drina-Posavina, has started to activate all people from Bosnia. The leader is one successful man from our region, and he now wants to set up a political party here with the people from our region. So, he is organizing an event [*Zavičajni dani*], for the third/forth time. But for me, I'm personally not that much interested in this organization because we have already our established networks and I know that someone who knows you for ten years or more will help you before someone you will meet now.

In Croatia, the situation was similar to Serbia, although some external BiH migrants have been members of organizations in this country. Most of their activism has been in different political parties. This is very common for those living in small cities, who find political engagement at the local level to be a very important aspect of their lives in the local municipality. Their engagement in a political party is frequently related to their personal and community needs. However, they still face various power relations and difficulties in achieving their main goals. A 42-year-old male BiH migrant, who has been politically active for many years said:

> It's clear that I have my goal, and that I agree with many things. Yes! And not just to go there for a pure individual interest. I'm always looking for a ways to help others and if I don't agree with something in my party, I clearly state that. I can't say that I feel discriminated, but I still haven't achieved any benefit from this membership. So, sometimes I just think about it. One more activity! That's it.

When reflecting on the informal networks among the different migrant groups in BiH, Serbia and Croatia it could be concluded that a large presence of informal networks among the migrant groups was not accompanied by high participation and membership in various local and home-town organizations. Participation in associations and groups in BiH was mostly by those with migrant experience who considered membership as an opportunity to advance their rights and status. A majority of the BiH external and internal migrants were members of different kinds of local organizations. According to their descriptions, membership in different organizations could be useful but the power relations and the groups' segregation usually limited the benefits from group membership, frequently depending on personal socioeconomic status and employment. Some success, regardless of personal socioeconomic characteristics, could be found in the hometown organizations but this was rather rare. In comparison, nonmigrants had not engaged in local organizations. The same was identified among the BiH external migrants in Croatia and Serbia. Although many were not members of existing hometown associations, they still organized their social lives around people in or from BiH. They considered their long-term networks with the population from BiH as the most important relationships in their everyday lives. Moreover, in both Croatia and Serbia there was an interest among the external migrants from BiH in membership in different political parties. They considered this as an important way to improve their position in the host countries.

Prosocial Behaviour and Collective Actions

Prosocial behaviour and collective action by individuals and groups are important aspects of social life and are likely to emerge only if a certain level of social capital already exists in a community (Grootaert *et al.*,

2004). For both relational and structural social capital, prosocial behaviour and collective actions for all three groups in focus were likely to be less than expected. In all three countries – BiH, Serbia and Croatia – the interviewees showed rather a low level of engagement in collective action but also a willingness to engage in collective action whenever there was a need or an opportunity for such involvement. Participation in collective action remained more voluntary and limited to humanitarian actions as well as those in a crisis situations, such as the period of floods in 2014. Collective actions should be considered by an overall assessment of the extent of willingness of people to cooperate and participate in group activities, as well as a through the type of activities undertaken collectively and its purpose. The purposes of collective actions might be different and depend on how community activities are organized. In some countries, these activities are the results of the political environment (Putnam, 2000). They might be politically oriented or serve some other public interest. In other contexts, collective actions might be voluntary and based on solidarity. These are usually oriented towards community goals and various humanitarian actions (Grootaert *et al.*, 2004).

In our research, the collective actions and prosocial behaviour of individuals have been approached by considering several aspects: civic engagement, willingness to help and general opinions about voluntary work, as well as participation in typical humanitarian or any other kind of voluntary activity and participation in collective or individual activities in crises, such as those organized around the floods in 2014 in particular. Each question was linked to the two dimensions of social capital: relational (trust and specific trust) and structural (networks and groups/associations).

In most of the interviews across BiH, Serbia and Croatia, all groups examined expressed willingness to help in general and whenever they have an opportunity to become involved. Although no particular explanation has been given, in many individual examples migrant experiences came up as a strong reason for engaging in collective actions. Almost all three groups were participating in some humanitarian actions, such as donating to socially disadvantaged groups and individuals via media services (messages via cell phones or phone calls for donations). A majority also shared a positive opinion about voluntary work although not many have actually been involved in it. Beside this, the interviews revealed a high level of participation in collective actions organized during the period of crisis – the natural flood disaster. Most of the interviewed population took part in the collective actions organized around the floods in 2014. These actions have been considered as the most important act of solidarity among these people regardless of their socioeconomic status, ethnicity or migrant experiences. However, the lack of general trust in institutions and people that was identified, as well as low participation in groups and associations, have strongly influenced further civic engagement. This has been based on a very negative opinions about the outcomes of some collective actions targeting the public good as well as some humanitarian actions. These findings are elaborated below.

All three groups in BiH expressed very positive views about helping people in general. This has been particularly important for the BiH external and internal migrants, who refer to their own migrant experience as a strong point and as a motivation for helping others. Moreover, most respondents have been taking a part in different humanitarian actions organized through media, such as humanitarian messages or phone calls, as well as initiating and participating in different humanitarian actions co-organized with the BiH diaspora. The comments of a 54-year-old male BiH external migrant in FBiH indicate this:

> I would help always, when I am in a situation to do so. I appreciate very much human-itarian and voluntary work, and I think there are lot of good humanitarian activities around my city. I don't do any voluntary work but when there is a humanitarian action in my city to help a sick child, I always participate. I mean to all people who need help. We usually get in touch with our diaspora, who is still very generous and willing to help! I've been also contacting them several times for different initiatives upon my return to Bosnia. There are still good people around.

However, in the same interview, as it was registered by many other BiH external migrants, general mistrust in institutions and people in BiH creates a lot of miscommunication and misunderstanding among the people. This is accompanied by a general socioeconomic status at the individual level:

> But, it is important that humanitarianism is not for private interest. I know some examples when people were looking after their own interests through these actions. I mean, I would always help, when I'm in the situation to do so. But, honestly, today less and less ... The economic situation is not encouraging you to think about helping another people.

Similar stories were recorded among BiH internal migrants. A majority of them had been engaged in various humanitarian actions and voluntary work. However, their reasons for engagement in both activities and their perceptions about them were quite different. Participation in humanitarian actions was based on a strong feeling of empathy for those in a marginal position. A BiH 46-year-old female internal migrant in FBiH related that:

> I'm always trying to help to people. I know how hard is to be without anything, trying just to survive. When we came here, we were depending just on the "good" people, on that if someone brings something to eat, gives us a place to stay, talk to us. That's why I try to help at any occasion. I'm not that much involved in some voluntary or humanitarian work but whenever I see an announcement for donating by phone call or SMS, I always participate. I just wish that I can do more, but the situation is not good and I'm struggling myself to survive and my family too.

At the same time the BiH internal migrants have different perceptions about voluntary work. A significant number see voluntary work as important for society, while at the same time they rather remain out of it. The data on this topic collected in the interviews might be summarized in the statement by a 40-year-old female internal migrant in RS:

> Volunteers are heroes for me. They are at the top position on my scale, really. Today, when 90% of population struggles with existential problems, to be a volunteer is equal to be a hero. I appreciate all kinds of volunteerism so much.

On the other hand, several internal migrants have seen voluntary work from another perspective. In several interviews it has been understood as a potential strategy for resolving their own socioeconomic situation. A 54-year-old female internal migrant in RS clearly explains her engagement in voluntary work for personal goals:

> I have been engaged in some voluntary work but I had a very bad experience. I mean, if you are a volunteer you should at least be stimulated by words and support and not to be treated as something "third rate" [*biti tretiran kao nešto treće*]. Maybe, someone came there to volunteer but some of us [she refers here to IDPs] were also thinking to get something more like a future job, finance, networks, and so on. I think that volunteer's work should be financially rewarded. Also, take example of my friend's sons, who have been looking for a job for years. They go to volunteer for months, and at the end, they are send back home. I think that voluntary work has been misused.

In addition to negative perceptions about the humanitarian and voluntary work, difficulty in proceeding with collective actions organized for the public good or the benefit of the broader community was recorded. This is linked to the overall lack of trust in institutions at all levels. Although it was identified mainly in the interviews with the nonmigrants in BiH, who were engaged in several collective actions at local levels, some internal and external migrants share the same opinion. This has been described by several participants in RS, who gather together with others in their neighbourhoods to advocate for community rights. Their collective action was not only stopped by local institutions but they were highly ethnicized and politicized in their means and goals:

> We get together here to defend the public space where our children have been playing since ever, which they ["local officials"] intend to use for other purposes. They have a plan to build a church here and in that case our children will lose the best space to play. We collected more than 5000 signatures and sent them to the local officials. We were hoping to get an opportunity to negotiate and discuss about this problem, because it is so important for our neighbourhood. But, the result is totally embarrassing. We haven't just been accused for our actions, we were also accused for being traitors of our own "ethnic group" [they refer here to the Serbian ethnic group]!! We are speechless! And, worried about future of our children and us here. How can we make any changes when they don't even care for the opinion of more than 5000 people.

In comparison to these negative perceptions about the collective actions – either humanitarian or for the public good – all three groups have a very positive opinion about the collective actions organized during the floods in BiH. They see this situation as the strongest evidence of the solidarity that emerged in BiH since the war period. Almost all interviewees from all three groups took part in the collective actions organized in BiH in 2014. They participated in various ways – in their local communities (*mjesne zajednice*), the media, social networks, jobs and in other ways. They participated in a variety of collective actions: evacuating people, cleaning houses, providing clothes and food, giving shelter and so on. For all groups interviewed, the floods were an example of people's solidarity regardless of their ethnicity, religion, class, education and other differences. This has been mentioned by members of all three groups as can be seen from the examples below. For example, a 47-year-old male BiH external migrant in FBiH stated:

> Just remembering the floods. All people helped, from all religious and ethnic groups. None ask you what's your name; everyone was helping everyone. I was driving trucks in a city with Croat population. We were donating them things they urgently needed, such as clothing and food. It was a nice moment when we [he refers to the Bosniacs ethnic group] got in the newspaper and TV with the Catholic priest, who was marking us as their saviours.

Similar statements were recorded by the internal migrants in RS. A 57-year-old male internal migrant in RS was involved in the collective actions during the floods with a high sense of empathy for the population who were exposed to the natural disaster:

> Of course, I was participating. I went immediately to apply for volunteering. I have such understanding for all people who lost their homes. I know how they feel. We, at least, had some help, I mean someone was giving us at least food, I remember it was Red Cross, and them [he refers here to people who were affected by the floods] what did they have? Nothing! I felt it is my obligation to help them, and I did.

Furthermore, for most of the nonmigrants the participation in the collective actions around the floods awoke certain memories of the times when they shared a common country, Yugoslavia, and the solidarity characterizing that period. Many of the people interviewed celebrated this collective action as a moment of victory in BiH, in contrast to the ongoing problems relating to ethnic and class division in contemporary BiH society. The following quote from a 50-year-old male nonmigrant reflects this:

> I can't explain how I was feeling in that period. We were all like one. Nothing was important, just to help people in the flooded areas. We were recruiting in the teams and every day sharing different assignments. Going to other cities to help. All people were engaged; artist, students, workers, managers, all. No one asked you who you are and what you do. Ethnicity wasn't a question at all. That reminded me of the old times, when we were building Yugoslavia through various actions [*radne akcije*]. So much solidarity among the people was again coming up, and I was truly thinking that we needed one disaster to happen to understand that war and all what have happened to us has nothing to do with people that we are the one!

However, as the comment below illustrates, willingness to participate in collective action is sometimes compromised due to the constant lack of trust in the institutions and people in BiH:

> But even that was in the end disrupted and politicized. Now, you just think who get all that humanitarian help collected around BiH. Who took all that money and so on. In this country, all finish always just around corruption. And I don't see any hope.

The BiH external migrants in Serbia expressed similar attitudes towards collective actions as did those in BiH. In part, the willingness to help and the positive perceptions about volunteerism and collective action are still based mainly on participation in humanitarian actions. Exceptions are noticed only in periods of crises, such as the floods in 2014 and support to refugees from Syria crossing through Serbia during 2015. In most of the interviews, their migrant experience is highlighted as an important factor in helping other people. Most of all, their personal experience of being refugees, without a home, has a strong influence on their engagement in these collective actions. Their opinions could be summarized through this comment by a 48-year-old female BiH external migrant, who came to Serbia as a refugee 20 years earlier:

> Yes, I would always help. I have always been helping by some donations and all other possibilities. I always call or send at least SMS whenever there is some humanitarian action. During the floods, I was volunteering and I went also to the places affected by the floods. You know, I always think about those people and remember my own experience when you in one moment stay without anything. You have no home, no money, nothing. You find yourself in the middle of nothing and on the road to nowhere. And than you need to start all over again, not just for yourself but also for your family. I just remember how even nice word meant a lot.

Similar stories were recorded by the BiH external migrants, who were engaged in humanitarian actions for the refugees from Syria and other countries. A 39-year-old male BiH external migrant in Serbia thinks that the humanitarian and voluntary work is very positive. In particular, he feels empathy with those who have been in the same situation that he and his family were in almost 20 years earlier. He sees the situation of refugees from Syria transiting through Serbia through this lens:

> That's why I'm also trying now to engage with these poor people from Syria. I applied as a volunteer to an organization here. We have been organizing different activities in the last months. Many of us are actually former refugees from BiH and Croatia. Well, for me, I see myself in them. It's not important what's your name and who you are. You just think how is to be alone on the road and how important is to survive, and you always survive just thanks to good people and their help. I remember my arrival here with my family. I was still small but I remember clearly how it was to live in the collective centres, waiting for some charity, and with destiny, which is so uncertain.

Experiences as migrants, but also positive integration experiences, play an important role for the BiH external migrants in Croatia. The majority were involved in different collective actions during the floods in BiH in order to help their families, friends and others affected by the floods. They also expressed the willingness to help, whenever there is a possibility to do so. According to a 51-year-old female BiH external migrant in Croatia, her neighbours were participating as much as she was in supporting her family affected by floods. All her neighbours contributed to support her family and places in BiH affected by the floods:

> My hometown was, unfortunately, affected by the floods very badly. My family came to me without anything!! It was really disaster to all of us. But, the people around engaged immediately and helped a lot! They were collecting cloths, money and other stuff. They were coming every day to ask if my family and friends in BiH needed anything. I'm really impressed and very happy with the people around me. My Croat neighbours, I mean. Everything is easy when you have your neighbour to rely on …

Participation in collective action by all three migrant groups in all three countries has been similar in many ways. In comparison to their perceptions about trust and participation in the networks and groups/associations, most the interviewees stressed the importance of collective actions. Collective action brought people together regardless of their socioeconomic, individual and cultural characteristics and migration experiences. This was particularly the case during the floods in BiH and Serbia in 2014, when most of the interviewees participated in the collective action around floods, either through helping personally or via various donations. Other cases of collective action were reported for different humanitarian causes. These humanitarian campaigns were mostly organized through media or private initiatives. For example, all three groups across the three countries described their participation in humanitarian initiatives such as donations through SMS messages. However, the initiatives in organizing or starting these activities were at rather a low level. The main reason was lack of trust in institutions and the complexity of social networks. Nevertheless, several initiatives at the local level, apart from those relating to the floods, are giving hope for more civic engagement of the population, regardless of their migrant status and other socioeconomic differences.

Conclusion

Our investigation identified the important role that social capital plays in the postconflict environment in the SEE region, even though this role is characterized by a number of complexities, obstacles and challenges.

All three groups that were studied – external BiH migrants, internal BiH migrants and nonmigrants – shared a common view that their everyday lives were sustained due to the social relationships within their "communities" and local municipalities rather than to state and government support. This indicates the importance of social capital in the everyday lives of citizens and migrants living in this region. To a certain extent this has already been confirmed by scholars who have focused on these issues in BiH and other parts of SEE region (e.g. Petrovic, 2007; Čapo and Halilovich, 2013).

Through detailed discussion of the multidimensional perspectives of social capital for these three demographic categories, this study has shown that the social relationships between the people were strongly affected by the economic and political transformation processes in the region, in addition to their migrant experiences. These imposed new social norms and social relations in the postconflict environment. For example, the relational dimension of social capital implies that a lack of general trust in institutions and people is common for all three groups and countries, while slight differences might exist at the local levels. The local level still plays the crucial role in organizing people's lives, while personal sociocultural characteristics such as education, ethnicity, religious, class and socioeconomic status are important in establishing and sustaining daily communication and various kinds of social networks. Consequently, based on these communications and networks, structural social capital largely replaces and compensates for the lack of trust in institutions in postconflict societies. At the same time, structural social capital indicates that migrant experiences, in terms of minority-majority relationships, ethnicity and the resulting feelings of exclusion for both migrant and nonmigrant groups, are important but not crucial in everyday lives. Migrant experiences might influence relationships at the individual or group/association level in terms of people's exclusion from the (re)settled places, but nonmigrants have the same perception. In that regard, people did not necessarily rely on their migrant and nonmigrant experiences in terms of solidarity or empathy in approaching various socioeconomic problems in the places where they (re)settled. Personal socioeconomic characteristics also play an important role, again raising the question of how social capital is transferred from individual to "community" level (Coleman, 1988) and distributed to all actors in society (Tzanakis, 2013).

Finally, collective action, perceived as the outcome of the relational and structural social capital, further complicates our understanding of social capital and migration given through the analysis of the collective actions during the crisis and noncrisis periods. The period of crisis, analysed through the floods in 2014, showed the existence of a high level of social capital regardless of differences among the three groups. At the same time, the noncrisis period rather lacks collective action because of difficulties in the political and institutional environment in these countries. Consequently, for any further engagement with social capital at the vertical level, such as potential for strong participation in associations and more cooperation in economic and social projects (Putnam, 2000), trust and civic engagement need to be developed further. For those reasons, it is important to understand collective actions better in the period of crisis and noncrisis as well as structural social capital and the features of informal networks.

The main message and policy implication from our analysis is that social capital still plays an extremely important role in integration processes of the selected communities. This message challenges the stereotypical belief that (re)establishing social relations in a postconflict environment is difficult and sometimes impossible. This analysis shows how people's livelihoods in postconflict environments is possible can be sustained due to the social capital emerging on daily basis within and between different population groups. Accordingly, policymaking should be focused on creating new potential for civic engagement at the local level while taking into consideration the elaborated dimensions of social capital with all their positive and negative aspects.

Bojana Babic

Social Capital and Ethnic Diversity – A Qualitative Investigation from the SEE Region

Introduction

Social capital has played an important role in the (re)integration processes of the migrant and nonmigrant populations in postconflict environments in Bosnia and Herzegovina (BiH), Serbia and Croatia. This is a general conclusion from the qualitative in-depth analysis of the multidimensional aspects of social capital in these countries (Chapter 3). Specifically, based on the collected data, we were able to identify that challenges in the political and economic environment – followed by a lack of trust in institutions and people – have been replaced by specific or particularized trust in certain individuals, institutions and social networks among all three migrant groups that were studied: external migrants, internal migrants and nonmigrants. The social networks built upon the trust in particular people and institutions, mainly at the local level, have had an important role in managing everyday livelihoods for all the three groups. However, the influence of these networks is limited due to newly established majority-minority relationships, often based on the ethnic structure of the country and other sociocultural characteristics and migrant experiences of all three groups.

These emerging social relationships and norms therefore require further investigation on the ground where they take place. Generally, in (re) building multiethnic societies in postwar environments, such as BiH, it is crucial to understand how ethnicity and ethnic diversity in changed heterogeneous and homogeneous ethnic environments influence social capital. Specifically, it is important to explore how ethnicity intersects with other sociocultural characteristics such as gender, age and class and how it operates in relation to the main dimensions of social capital: trust, networks and prosocial actions. This chapter addresses these issues in a systematic manner. First, it introduces the main theoretical features and links between ethnicity and the different dimensions of social capital. Second, it continues to explore the main literature, which focuses on social capital and ethnicity in BiH in particular. Third, it briefly describes the sample on which the discussion of the results is based. Finally, the discussion of results is presented through four case studies, focused on both homogeneity and heterogeneity (the majority and minority ethnic group relationships) environments for all three groups in focus – BiH external migrants, internal migrants (IDPs) and nonmigrants – across three different SEE countries: Banja Luka (RS-BiH), Bugojno (FBiH-BiH), Novi Sad (Serbia) and Plaški (Croatia).

Ethnicity and Social Capital in Theory

The majority of studies that we reviewed have focused on the link between trust and ethnicity (see, for example, Putnam, 2000 and Halpern, 2005) and frequently indicate a negative association between them (Alesina and La Ferrara, 2005; Costa and Kahn, 2003; Marshall and Stolle, 2004). The feelings of "threat" from outsiders with regard to limited resources leads to distrust and intolerance towards outsiders and increased solidarity within one's own group (Blumer, 1954; Giles and Evans, 1985; Bowyer, 2009). The dominant groups are frequently more trusted than minorities (Uslaner, 2002). Ethnic diversity, therefore, might create a feeling of more security among people with a similar ethnic background (McPherson *et al.*, 2001) and mobilize further political actions towards other ethnic groups (Oliver, 2001). Putnam explains this phenomenon as distancing from the collective life of the members of different ethnic groups in general ("hunkering down") (Putnam, 2007), while other scholars see it as a potential for ethnicity to lead people to ignore inequality and conflict in society in general (Stolle and Hooghe, 2005; Hero, 2007). The former explanation appears mainly in Putnam's view of social capital seen in the broader societal context and emphasizing the importance of the collective value of social networks in building democracy and collective oriented societies (Putnam, 1993). Putnam sees that individual and structural trust provide multiple positive consequences for collective action, democratic governance and economic performance. For example, at the individual level, social trust is associated with volunteering, donating to charity, tolerance and other forms of prosocial behaviour (Sonderskov, 2011; Uslaner, 2002) and is characteristic of more democratic environments. Structurally, the societies with greater trust are characterized by more effective collective decision making, better demographic government and higher economic growth (Knack and Keefer, 1997; Knack, 2002; Bjornskov, 2009). Under these circumstances ethnicity is less important. According to the defenders of the social inequality approach to ethnicity and social capital, access to the social capital remains rather limited to membership of privileged groups and networks. These groups and networks function primarily for economic purposes and power relations, ethnicity being of lesser importance. The exclusiveness of the privileged groups and networks perpetuates advantages and disadvantages and inequality (Bourdieu, 1980; Portes, 1998). This is the exclusionary side of social capital (Gauntlet, 2011), where social capital is used to produce and reproduce inequality, which supports social stratification (Bourdieu, 1983). Trust, then, might emerge as a crucial dimension in the relationship between ethnicity and social capital, as trust frequently appears as both a cause and effect of that relationship. However, this might be a perception rather than a fact, as is described below.

A number of studies emphasize that trust has been an overemphasized dimension of social capital in the context of its relationship with ethnicity (Hooghe, 2007; Semenas, 2014). Instead of focusing primarily on trust, they suggested that social networks should be prioritized in discussions about the role of ethnicity in social capital. Among various reasons for this, the literature argues that "informal sociability" (based mostly on the daily communication white the neighbourhoods, work place, public spaces, and so on) is the most accessible to the wider population. Through informal sociability, individuals might be less sensitive to ethnic diversity than trust (Hooghe, 2007; Letki, 2008). This might create opportunities to adjust to reciprocal obligations among friends and neighbours as members of the same community regardless of their ethnicity or other sociocultural differences (Letki, 2008). For example, place-related features such as friendliness, ease of interaction, the nature of public space and the accessibility of local events and amenities might enhance and extend social networks even in ethnically diverse environments (Worpole and Knox, 2007; Halilovich, 2012). In such circumstances, the bridging effects between different ethnic groups might provide better social environments for collective life

(Putnam, 1995). That, however, might not be the case for the formal associations and groups, which are an important feature of the various forms of civil engagements and networking. Formal associations and groups are frequently linked to socioeconomic status and they usually gather those with similar sociocultural characteristics, such as well-educated individuals, as members (Li *et al.*, 2005), or they are linked to ethnicity, gender, race and status. Their memberships are usually limited by their structure, size and interests or goal orientation. Hence, although formal associations and groups bring various benefits to their members (Coleman, 1988), they might also enforce various kinds of inequalities, including those based on ethnicity. The performance of the formal as well as informal networks therefore is not easily separated from trust, either at the individual level or the structural level. Moreover, the ambivalent relationships between the trust and reciprocity and people's attitudes of (in)formal networking, might bring rather tiny investment in formal social networks, as both require stronger collective framework and actions (Putnam, 2007).

It might, therefore, be difficult or challenging for collective life and its potential for collective action to emerge in ethnically diverse environments. If collective action only appears when a certain level of social capital is built from trust and networks, its link to ethnic diversity might be negative. In other words, ethnic diversity is likely to damage the ability of such societies to create and maintain public goods (Easterly *et al.*, 1997; Miguel and Gadgetry, 2005; Ruttan, 2006), which are needed for common goals and actions at the broader societal level. The reason for this is that ethnic diversity might enforce cooperation tied to an ethnic group itself rather than between different ethnic groups, strengthening reciprocity within the ethnic group (Fehr and Gachter, 2002; Nowak and Sigmund, 2005). As a result, an increase in ethnic diversity might diminish the possibilities for cooperation among individuals with different ethnic backgrounds (Waring, 2011). According to Waring (2011), this can lead to ethnic dominance, both within and between different ethnic groups, which then additionally complicates collective actions. The ethnic dominance is not only based on ethnic social identity but it endogenously involves other social differences such as class, gender and race (Horowitz, 2002). Hence, the effects of the intergroup relations directly influence cooperation between different groups and their potential for their collective actions. Some scholars have suggested that the main difficulty is testing collective action and ethnic dominance, because this requires the existence of minimum ethnic diversity

(Collier, 2002; Waring, 2011). At the same time, some studies show that ethnic diversity and dominance should be rather observed in broader socioeconomic circumstances, such as periods of natural disasters, other crises or simply informal gathering oriented towards common society interests in the period of certain crises. In postdisaster recovery situations, for example, collective action replaced formal assistance and the lack of economic resources (Aldrich, 2010) regardless of ethnic diversity in the society. More evidence about potential of collective action in postdisaster recovery contexts has been presented in the literature (e.g. Polletta and Jasper, 2001; Aldrich, 2010). According to these studies, collective action provides the best results in the period of crises, when any form of differences is less important compared to everyday life needs. Yet, it remains to consider the link between ethnicity and social capital as a straightforward process even for the circumstances of crises or other forms of needs for urgent solidarity actions. This can be seen in the following review of the literature about postwar recovery efforts in Bosnia and Herzegovina, together with a study about the contemporary relationships between ethnicity and social capital in that country.

Ethnic Diversity and Social Capital in Bosnia and Herzegovina

Bosnia and Herzegovina illustrates both the importance and difficulty of addressing issues of ethnic diversity and social capital. In the postwar recovery period, the lack of an effective institutional environment has frequently been replaced by various informal networks and the social relationships emerging on the ground. However, (re)building the prewar multiethnic society in BiH remains a rather long-term process for several compelling reasons. On one hand, painful economic and political processes have been complicated by ethnically based institutional divisions within the country (Biber, 2010; Efendic and Hadziahmetovic, 2015). On the other hand, the prewar multiethnic (multicultural) environments have been affected by new emerging majority and minority relationships on the ground (confirmed by census data in 2016) and other sociocultural characteristics such as differences in migrant status, class and employment.

Moreover, in BiH the differing status of migrants – such as external BiH migrants, internal BiH migrants (IDPs) and nonmigrants – as well as ethnicity, have been overlapping in a number of different ways. During the

1992–1995 Bosnian war, some 2.2 million people changed their place of origin, either as external migrants or IDPs (Efendic *et al.*, 2014). In addition to more than 1 million of those who fled the country, around 1.1 million were internally displaced between the RS and FBiH. This created new social "realities" all over the country and new division based on the majority and minority relationships in previously ethnically diverse communities (homogeneous and heterogeneous). Majorities are usually considered those who belong to predominant ethnic group in a particular region or municipality – interchangeably Bosniacs, Serbs or Croats in different parts of the country, regardless their migrant experience and status. At the same time, in these "new" communities, minorities are considered those with different ethnic background along those with certain migrant experiences such as returnees (external BiH migrants) or nonmigrants with different ethnic background, as well as IDPs with the same ethnic background as the ethnic majority. This is the case in most of the "micro societies" in BiH, notified in both entities FBiH than in RS. The ethnic division is further complicated by the continuing difficulty of economic and political transformation across the country. In BiH, close to 50% of the workforce is formally unemployed and a large proportion of the workforce (estimated to be around 30%) works informally. The political transition rather lags behind the initial initiative to establish a democratic society and political tensions still continue to be present throughout the country.

The different majority and minority social relationships that emerged in this complicated environment have been a research interest in a number of studies in BiH. According to this literature (e.g. Capo and Halilovich, 2013), the prewar relationships and networks might be interrupted by a new minority-majority relationships at the local level as well as at the national level but not necessarily with negative connotation. For example, Porobic and Mameledzija (2013) report how bringing and bonding social capital played important role for the returnees (external BiH migrants of Bosniac ethnic group) on their return to mainly homogenous (Serbian) ethnic environments. Both the interethnic group's relationships and ethnically diverse groups' relationships have functioned positively in certain local municipalities. Similar findings were registered by Petrovic (2007), who provides an example of recovery of prewar local multiethnic ties and trust within the neighbourhoods in a small semiurban area. At the same time, a number of other researchers identified the existence of rather negative social relationships between those who fled the country and those who stayed behind (Kaya, 2009; Halilovich, 2013b). Others pointed to the difficulty in (re)building prewar relationships and networks due to different migration experiences (Povrzanovic-Frykman, 2003; Stefansson, 2004) and the new emerging socioeconomic status of the various groups.

At the same time, the social networks built up from below have not encountered a favourable structural environment. Porobic and Mameledzija (2013) pointed out that returnees' organizations for minority groups, despite their work and enthusiasm, have failed to develop further due to the lack of political and institutional efforts to support (re)integration processes. The emerging social networks between returnees and the rest of the population at the local level are still not influential and require further political empowerment of the returnees through the promotion of active citizenship. A more overall structural perspective on the social capital has been given by an UNDP study (2009). Elaborating on the potential of social capital for poverty reduction, this study concludes that social relationships have been affected more by new emerging class and labour divisions (rich versus poor or management versus workers) than ethnicity. At the same time, the study acknowledges that those with migration experience, such as returnees and IDPs, often suffer more from social isolation and therefore have less access to social capital. According to the findings, family ties and their different inclusion and exclusion potential, remain at the core of their social networks (UNDP, 2009). For example, personal and family connections have a crucial role in social networks and exclusion as they channel access to most public goods. Moreover, along with the political struggles, these networks also reduce the potentials for membership of associations and for voluntary work (UNDP, 2009).

In addition to the structural obstacles in the relationship between ethnicity and social capital, Popova (2009) points to the potential origin of this situation. In her extensive study on the role of social capital for postconflict reconstruction in BiH, Popova (2009) identified the failures of various international actors to address the importance of rebuilding social capital. She stressed that new institutional ethnic divisions within the country worsen the possibility for social capital to form at the macro level as well as the difficulty of promoting the concept of citizenship in form of a social contract with the state. To encourage people to become active participants in rebuilding BiH requires recognition of the pre-existing multiethnic relationships and the way in which they might be recovered through a bottom-up approach – as the institutional, political and economic environment have not been favourable for this (Popova, 2009).

We aim to add to the body of qualitative research about social capital and migration by exploring how ethnicity and social capital have been negotiated on the ground in different ethnic environments in BiH. In extensive research about three dimensions of social capital – trust (general and specific), networks (informal and groups/associations) and collective actions of three different groups (external migrants, internal migrants and nonmigrants) – we find that the importance of the ethnicity for the social capital emerges. Informal networking has mainly compensated for the low level of general and specific trust, participation in the groups and associations and collective actions. This situation is the result of the common determinants that link all three groups: economic-political environment, migrant status, ethnicity and other sociocultural characteristics. However, how ethnicity has been interacting with migrant status and other sociocultural characteristics such as class, gender, age, employment status and housing, still remains unclear. Specifically, for the majority and minority relationship in the postwar heterogeneous and homogeneous environments, ethnicity represents a part of everyday personal identity among individuals and groups. It is important for societies undergoing transition because certain socioeconomic and historical circumstances can contribute to it becoming politicized and hence becoming a potential conflict-generating factor (Rothschild, 1981). However, it is also able to prevent this. We looked at how ethnicity and three dimensions of social capital – trust, networks and collective actions – have been negotiated between majority and minority ethnic groups through their everyday lives in homogenous and heterogeneous social environments for three groups: external BiH migrants, internal BiH migrants (IDPs) and nonmigrants. In particular, we pay attention to the intersection of migrant status and the main socio-economic factors such as employment, housing and civil society engagements as well as the time dimension of the prewar and postwar periods. The discussion of the results is guided by 100 interviews and presented thorough four case studies of homogenous and heterogeneous ethnic environments: Banja Luka (RS-BiH), Bugojno (FBiH-BiH), Novi Sad (Serbia) and Plasko (Croatia).

A Note on Ethnicity

Ethnicity presents one of the most complex and vague socially categories and it is frequently put into the context of religion, nationality, race, language, region or "minority". Its close link to identity politics and nation state further complicates the integration of ethnicity in civil society and everyday lives. The definition of ethnicity ranges from various attempts to consider ethnicity as given (premordialist, modernist, transactionalist, social psychological perspective, rational choice perspective, the ethno-symbolic approach and the modern anthropological approach) to the preference of socially constructed values, beliefs and behaviours. Each of these definitions and interpretations influence how people understand the ethnicity in the broader social context and arrangements. For example, if ethnicity is considered as given, like blood, myths about kinship and common origin, then it might easily be linked to nationals idea of citizenship and "naturally" formed community. This further leads to the notion of ethnicity as a privilege for individuals, groups and elites, enabling them to obtain benefits from belonging to an ethnic group, including material (Lake and Rothschild, 1998) or nonmaterial advantages (Ross, 1982) and used for different political and economic purposes.

In order to address the differences in the interpretation of ethnicity, a further understanding of ethnicity and ethnic identities have been linked to literature on culture and cultural forms, such as idealization of the past, language modification and religion identification (Armstrong, 1982). Culture appears as the most common link with ethnicity and can be a replacement for the class-structure division of society (Eriksen, 1993). In that regard, it is important to note that cultural differences are often linked to complex political, economic and social structures. According to Eriksen (1993), cultural differences will become identity factors when they are socially relevant; in other words, the ethnic element of identity might be incorporated into personal identities only when it provides individuals with certain benefits (something "valuable"), both material and nonmaterial. Ethnic identity hence becomes most important when it becomes a mechanism for bonding community members and generating togetherness (Popova, 2009), or when it is threatened.

It might then be observed that in order to encompass broader material, political or symbolic environments, the ethnicity should be put into the relationships with other social categories such as class, sex, age and relevant status, such as migrant, employment and housing. A number of anthropologists point out that social identities are segmentary and a person might simultaneously be a member of family, local community and of an ethnic group (Popova, 2009). As such, the multiple-individual identities, including class, gender, education, age and others, can stand on their own interesting flows and might prioritise ethnic identities to become group-forming factors when required. This might provide a better understanding of intergroup relationships and social networks in terms of various conflicts, inequalities or the majority-minority dichotomy as well as heterogeneous-homogenous; inclusion-exclusions, or inside-outside relationships. Building upon this observation, we refer to ethnicity as one of the most important features for the multiple cultural and political identities of the three groups in focus – BiH external migrants, IDPs and nonmigrants – and present people's own stories and perceptions about meaning of ethnicity in their own lives.

Data and Sample

The sample for this discussion comes from the qualitative research elaborated in the previous chapters and includes three different migrant groups: external migrants – (i) ex-diaspora returnees, external BiH migrants to Serbia and Croatia; (ii) BiH internal migrants (IDPs) and (iii) nonmigrants. The sample is based on 100 interviews: 60 interviews in BiH (20 domiciles/nonmigrants; 20 internal migrants; 20 external migrants), with 20 additional interviews with BiH external migrants in Serbia and 20 in Croatia. In framing our sample, particular attention was given to the role of ethnicity, with the aim of representing all ethnicities in the sampled areas. The data were collected through fieldwork conducted in the period between April and September 2015. The fieldwork included a pilot questionnaire, a semistructured questionnaire, participant observation and a number of informal talks with members of all three groups. Moreover, to understand how ethnicity is negotiated among the majority and minority ethnic groups in the homogenous and heterogeneous social environments, the results are presented by focusing on four case studies: Banja Luka (RS BiH), Bugojno (FBiH), Novi Sad (Serbia) and Plaški (Croatia). The description of the results includes the link between ethnicity and three dimensions of social capital: trust, networks and collective action. It is accompanied by a short description of general observations of each case study followed by individual stories from the field for all three groups in focus.

Discussion of Results

Banja Luka

Banja Luka is the main administrative centre and the largest urban area in the entity of Republika Srpska, in BiH. With its population of around 200 000, the Serbian ethnic group counts as the majority, constituting around 90% of the population; the ethnic minorities of Bosniacs and Croats make up around 4% and 3% respectively. With the Serbian population increasing (from 55% in 1991 to 95% according to 2013 census data), the ethnic harmony and composition existing before 1990s has been affected in multiple ways. Although the city avoided direct military engagement, unlike many other major cities in BiH such as Sarajevo and Mostar, the majority of Bosniacs and the Croat population left the city during the 1990s, while their religious institutions (Muslim mosques and Catholic churches) were damaged or completely destroyed. Those returning to the city encountered a number of difficulties and the population of these two groups is much lower numbers than it was before the war (there were around 45% of the both ethnic groups in 1991). At the same time, due to the effects of the war, the city changed its character. Thousands of Banja Luka Bosniacs and Croats have been replaced by thousands of Serb internal refugees (IDPs), some from Croatia and some from other areas of BiH where Bosniacs or Croats represent majority groups. A lot of those new settlers came from rural areas and were not used to living in an urban environment. Banja Luka always had a proud, perhaps even snobbish class of "old Banja Luka" residents who were inclined to look down at these peasant newcomers "with mud on their boots". Some of the incoming refugees, for their part, resented the cosmopolitanism of the "old Banja Luka" residents who, they suspected, might rather see the old Bosniacs and Croats than newcomer Serbs living in Banja Luka (Cockburn *et al.*, 2001). This previously industrial centre has become the administrative centre of the RS entity, where the majority of population is looking for employment opportunities. The rest is frequently engaged in the informal economy or self-styled employment. These economic difficulties are further fostered by political tensions between the leading and opposition political groups (including minorities).

In that environment, it is not surprising that all three dimensions of social capital and ethnicity for the three groups in focus might be described as complex and difficult. The majority of interviews conducted among all three groups in Banja Luka linked ethnicity to confirmed lack of trust in the institutions and people at the national level, but often at the local level too. Those with better economic and employment performance have greater trust in the local government – here ethnicity might intersect differently with migrant status for the majority and minority ethnic groups. For IDPs and nonmigrants, seen as part of the majority ethnic group, migrant status and personal sociocultural characteristics are important features of their trust in the local institutions. Hence, IDPs and nonmigrants with better employment status and economic performance might be seen as the main threat to social capital within the majority ethnic group, where ethnicity appears as an important element for social capital only if the majority group is threaten at the national level. This behaviour is evident even in informal and formal networking within the majority ethnic group. The interest-based attitudes within the majority ethnic group is characteristic for the many individuals involved in this research, but it is not necessarily an essential feature. There are several exceptions where solidarity and reciprocity relationships based either as local diasporic or neighbourhood aspects might overcome potential ethnic tensions and exclusions. A number of IDPs conduct their lives mainly with IDPs from the same place of origin, while a number of nonmigrants and BiH external migrants have kept strong local bonds regardless of different ethnicity (Halilovich, 2012). However, BiH external migrants perceive that ethnicity is still one of the biggest obstacles to their full participation in local institutional and social life and consequently they display a lack of trust in the municipal and also national services. In fact, many of the interviewees think that ethnicity has priority over other sociocultural characteristics such as education, gender, age, or employment status. That reflects strong intergroup relationships and makes informal and formal network fully based on solidarity and reciprocity. Yet, several cases of the gender discrimination of different ethnically based NGOs confirmed that gender and power relations are characteristic for all ethnic groups in the city and that they might be important obstacle, but also initiative for multiethnic-group collaboration. There are various examples where women with different ethnic background collaborate in the case of common economic and gender interests. Moreover, the number of examples of daily practices between different ethnic groups confirms that. Particularly in urban neighbourhoods good social interactions and networking have emerged from below. This has been confirmed by several cases of collective action in the city. The best examples are responses to the countrywide spread of floods in 2014, where not only the ethnically mixed neighbourhoods but all residents of the city became involved in helping each other and those most affected regardless of their ethnic background. The examples described below illustrate these cases. They are narrated by members of the majority ethnic group (IDPs and nonmigrants) and the minority ethnic group (BiH external migrants).

An interview with a Serbian couple, a 54-year-old male and external BiH migrant, and his wife, a 42-year-old IDP, and many other interviews, confirms that being a member of the majority ethnic group in Banja Luka today does not guarantee you any privileges. After more than 20 years, this couple is still living in a rented apartment and they are still out of the official labour market. Upon their arrival in the city, they considered their membership of the majority Serbian ethnic group as their main resource to resolve the employment and housing problems. They immediately engaged with political and civic organizations with the aim of participating in the development of postwar Banja Luka and the RS. However, over time the situation worsened and today they consider "ethnicity" to be a privilege just for certain networks and people:

> After 20 trials of forced movements from our apartment [*delozacija*] we are still living in a rented apartment [...]. Why this anymore, when I put myself in all possible political parties and support the initial idea of development of RS? I came here from Croatia and I immediately engaged with the main Serbian politics here. But, until now I didn't have any benefit from that. At the end, I realized that "they" [the Serbian leading political parties] call you just for elections to collect the votes for them. I do that because I need money but all my hopes to have their help for permanent job and to resolve my housing problem have fallen apart. In my eyes, all these religious and ethnic leaders are the worst criminals. You have to be "a part of the criminal network" and we [he and his wife] don't want that.

This participant considers that main problem for this situation was his rejection to be a part of the corrupted system built up on the nationalist vision and material-end based needs. That led him and his wife to look for other networks in the city. In the same interview, his wife, a 42-year-old IDP with secondary education background, narrated their experience of their struggles to make a minimal livelihood since they met in Banja Luka. For her, informal employment and collaboration with other women, including those with different ethnic background, became the only possible way to survive in this city. After years of struggle to achieve a certain level of social and economic security she became disappointment in the local institutions. She had a little more success with gender-based networks:

> I thought that my engagement in a Serbian organization would bring me new opportunities [...]. Now I am managing thanks to a Bosniac friend [an external BiH migrant and a member of the minority ethnic group] and her organization. We met by coincidence and since then we continue helping each other with various businesses matters.

The difficulty in building up the reciprocity and solidarity within the majority Serbian ethnic group in Banja Luka in the homogenous ethnic environment has not precluded interpersonal informal and formal networking. Narratives of the social relationships within the Serbian ethnic group are seen mostly as overlapping between ethnicity, politics and personal goals. For those with better employment positions, ethnicity is either a tool to achieve a certain goal and a less important feature among those who share the economic and political power. For example, some NGO's preoccupied with the problems of the IDPs shows how the initial ideas of networking based on addressing common problems and interests later failed as a result of the personal interests of individuals and power-based relationships between the members in the organization. The initial work of this organization targeted the main socioeconomic problems of the IDPs in RS, such as housing, employment and social integration in the city of Banja Luka. Another 42-year-old female employee in the government of RS and a 58-year-old male employee in the City of Banja Luka agree that among their circles ethnicity has not an important role, as he states:

> I don't see that ethnicity matters a lot at my workplace. We are people with high education and good position, so we are practically belonging to a "higher" class of society and we actually try to help each other to maintain and improve our "positions".

For a number of IDPs, in-group conflicts within the majority ethnic groups might appear not only because of education and employment status but also due to their limited participation in the local institutions. Sometimes, they feel oppressed by the nonmigrants due to their migrant status. However, they all agree that the "borders" of their majority ethnic groups should be protected if any threat from outside were to come. The words of 62-year-old male IDPs show how that functions on the ground:

> We have to remain solid and together. It is important for us to defend our ethnicity and protect ourselves. I mean primarily in the national context because it seems to me that we might be seriously threaten at the national level. The lack of trust for institutions and people in BiH for me is primarily based on ethnicity […]. I can't say the same for the local level. We are feeling isolated in terms of political participation. In our local community [*mjesna zajednica*] nonmigrants are dominating and we are not able to rise our voices. They simply keep us "invisible", when it comes to our participation in decision making. We suddenly become "others".

The situation among the nonmigrants is likely to confirm the view that intergroup power relationships are based not only on the sociocultural characteristics of individuals but also on their migrant status. For nonmigrants in everyday life, ethnicity is less important than local belonging, which sometimes makes them more closed to the IDPs than to the minority Bosniac ethnic group. The words of the number of nonmigrants clarify this statement. For example, a 56-year-old male nonmigrant in Banja Luka said:

> The new people came here and change this city a lot. I'm still very much impressed how strong networks are among them and how they are helping each other. You can't practically find a job here if you are not a member of an IDPs group! I can say the same for my "old Serbian friends", who became important politicians and forgot their previous lives […]. My relationships with the returned Bosniacs neighbours are great as they have always been […]. For sure, they also keep themselves more tied to each other, but also they don't refuse to help others.

Collective action within the old and new neighbourhoods have been confirmed by a number of nonmigrants as well as IDPs and external BiH migrants. They presumed that local neighbourhood and everyday life experiences have often been able to overcome any potential ethnic and other socioeconomic-based division with the majority and minority groups in Banja Luka. There are several examples that show how this has happened on the ground, including several protests over public spaces in Banja Luka as well as collective action during the floods in 2014. A 50-year-old official representative of a local community (*mjesna zajednica*) recalls this:

> Yes, I would certainly say that people in Banja Luka still show much solidarity and feelings for the city itself. I would agree that ethnicity and politics overlaps many times but are not always the only bordering line for its residence and there are various examples that tied people despite any possible difference between them. Floods in 2014 are the best example. The whole city was volunteering. Then, we have several examples of people's demonstrations of months continuing fight over the public space, which gather together people of all ethnic groups and more independent political believes. That should be the moment that shows how democratic society is still possible.

The importance of these collective actions and voluntary based activities has been confirmed by the majority of the external BiH migrants in Banja Luka. Without exception, they all agree that floods in 2014 reminded them of the old "gold times" of the city's prewar multicultural charter. However, that has not changed a lot in terms of their daily struggles in the city. They presented their difficulties as being members of minority ethnic group both in relationship to the majority ethnic group as well as intergroup minority relationships. A 47-year-old external BiH migrant explained that returning to Banja Luka was not an easy task. She confirms that even today she feels like a member of a minority group but mainly in regards to the general political and social environment rather than to people she engages with on everyday basis. She sees that the lack of general trust to local institutions is very much linked to her position as a returnee, but also to her ethnicity. Her opinion is built on different experiences in engagement in the local government and civil society after her return:

> I don't feel oppressed here in Banja Luka, and I communicate with all people here. However, I do think that our status as returnees in Banja Luka is not good at all. On our return, I was engaging in all possible organizations just to get employment. I also was a member of a political party on behalf of my "local community" [*mjesna zajednica*]. I was selected because I was representing Bosniacs minority group within Serbian political party. I gave maximum from my side in that but after the elections were finished, none even asked about me anymore. So, I gave up and totally lost any trust to local authorities […]. Now, I'm just using some of those contacts for helping other external migrants [mainly diaspora members] to resolve their problems when they are coming here during the summer […]. It is still important "who" you are, even after all these years.

For many other returnees in Banja Luka the vision of joining forces towards local (re)integration through the various ethnically based NGOs has been present over the years. Moreover, the Bosniac returnees have been recognized as a minority group in the city and were granted public spaces and funding for establishing NGOs, which should foster their (re)integration in the city. However, the destiny of these organizations has been very different and has been similar to other forms of groups and associations. Power relations played an important role in their work. One example is a gender-focused NGO, which was formed by a group of external and internal migrant Bosniac women. Their organization gathers women of all classes, education levels, ages and employed in different ways. The main purpose is to provide help to other Bosniac women who suffer from the lack of job opportunities and social engagements in the city. However, after 2 years of successful work, the organization was closed due to in-group out-group conflicts. Power relations within the association and minority in-group emerged. According to a 50-year-old member of an NGO, the end of their organization was sad moment for all:

> It was the heart of our social lives and hopes. We were just waiting for the moment to go there […]. After a while, many tensions between the leaders emerged, lots of them were accused of mismanagement of the money coming to the organization. The situation by the time got worse. But, I think that the main problem came from the outside. As minority group in Banja Luka we got an office for our activities. But unfortunately, other members of our group [she refers here to male members], were judging our work a lot and decided to take from us the office.

A successful example of a Bosniac women's organization established as a part of a larger group of Bosniac women's organizations around the country indicates that the relationship between social capital and ethnicity in Banja Luka is not as straightforward as the previous example might suggest. According to the words of their leader, a 52-year-old Bosniac woman, the main reason for their success is a common interest to support Bosniac women and their children to (re)integrate into the schools in Banja Luka and excellent cooperation with organizations around BiH. Moreover, the organization helped a number of young Bosniacs to obtain scholarships for their further education as well as access to the job market:

> I got to know this organization on my arrival here, when I had faced a number of difficulties with my children to (re)integrate in the schools. We returned here from Germany and we suddenly found ourselves to be 'minority' in our own city. Children

faced a number of problems, my husband decided to exclude himself from all problems and I found myself lonely in all that. Without job, without help, nothing [...]. I became a member of this organization and step by step I resolved all my major problems. Thanks to this membership I got a job in the RS Government, as a representative of the minority Bosniacs group. I'm now running this organization and I'm giving my best to improve our position in Banja Luka [...]. I think that ethnicity is still the main obstacle, and politics is all [...]. You have to be engaged in politics, otherwise you don't exist. That's why I represent Bosniacs' political interests here.

Bugojno

In comparison to Banja Luka and its ethnically homogenous environment characterized, by the dominance of the Serbian majority over the Bosniac minority, Bugojno presents one of the few heterogeneous societies in BiH and it contains a mixture of Bosniacs and Croats. The municipality is located in FBiH and the urban area itself contains around 25 000 people, of which the ethnic Bosniacs (42%) and Croats (35%) dominate the others (mostly Serbs). The prewar ethnic structure of the population has not changed that much, with the exception of the smaller Serbian population today. According to the rather limited statistics and despite the lack of any research about this city, the official number of returnees is estimated to be about 9000 people. Most of them have returned to the urban areas, which by that time became even more divided between the two main ethnic groups in the city. This division is enforced at both social and institutional level of everyday life in this community. A number of public places such as schools and kindergartens are ethnically divided and that threatens to reinforce the ethnic tensions instead of eventual reintegration. The same is found in the labour market and municipal services and institutions, which are influenced by ethnicity and membership of political parties. The economic struggles in the municipality and the difficulties in finding employment outside the bureaucracy make the situation in this still heterogeneous community very difficult.

Given these circumstances, social capital suffers not only from a lack of trust in national and local institutions, but also from the informal and formal networking. From the majority of interviews conducted among all three groups in focus in Bugojno, ethnicity is reported to be strongly linked to all three dimensions of social capital, regardless of our respondents' migrant status. The same might not be claimed for the sociocultural characteristics of the members of both groups. Intergroup relationships are still under the influence of the sociocultural characteristics that influence constantly increasing economic inequality within the two predominant ethnic groups. For example, many Bosniac nonmigrants see themselves excluded from even their own neighbourhoods because of their class and employment status frequently followed by their lack of the necessary political contacts. The same is confirmed by the IDPs and BiH external migrants, who have a lower socioeconomic status and no access to political power. The same stories are also found within the Croat ethnic group. Although the situation within this ethnic group might be slightly better, the intergroup conflicts have not disappeared. Sociocultural characteristics and political activism are important when it comes to opportunities to gain employment and other important issues.

Besides the erosion of informal networking, formal associations and organizations, struggles around the collective actions were also mentioned. Much of the volunteering work and various humanitarian actions are organized though religious organizations, with the only exception being during the floods in 2014. Impressions of the situation on the ground are presented further in the text with several examples from the two main ethnic groups (Bosniacs and Croats) in this heterogeneous environment.

According to a Bosniac IDPs family in Bugojno, the ethnic division of the city makes their livelihoods harder than one could ever expect. Since their arrival in this city, the problems around employment and housing had become more complicated due to the ethnic tensions and political unrest between the two leading ethnic political parties. Initially, they perceived their participation in a political party as a potential way to resolve the emerging issues that they were encountering in their lives. That has not yet happened and the family is managing on its own with the support from its extended family. According to a 53-year-old man, this is very hard task if one takes into consideration how ethnicity guides everyday lives in this small community:

> Since we came here it's been very hard to keep on track with our own lives. We tried to find a job in the public services, because this is the best way to be employed. You have all security. Some people advised us to become politically active and that this would provide us with jobs. But I understood that even politics is not for everyone [...]. I mean being in politics doesn't guarantee you any success, at least not to all. It's not that you come among your "own people" and that you are resolving all your problems [...]. In the end, we ended up in the informal sector. I'm doing all from

seasonal agricultural work to the physical work around the city. For that position all these stories about ethnicity and politics do not matter, trust me.

The struggles of the in and out-group ethnic relationship in Bugojno was narrated by other IDPs, including those from the opposite ethnic groups. A 48-year-old Croat female came to Bugojno to establish a new life with her family. She was familiar with the place from before because she had relatives in this city. Her frequent visits to the city in the prewar periods had influenced her decision to choose this city as a place to continue her life in BiH after becoming displaced. However, a number of disappointments emerged along with the years of struggles to maintain daily livelihoods in this community:

> I would never imagine that this city would become such as hard place to live in. I came here with my family because we believed that things would be much easier for us among family and friends here [...]. Well, I can't say that they were not of help but the things seemed to be becoming worse and worse. We still keep good relationships with all our neighbours but somehow you are forced to be directed to your own ethnic group. Here everyone follows where you go, where you eat, what you do, and so on. Your life is an open book and you are forced to behave within that framework. At least that gives some chances to survive.

The interviews with three nonmigrants families revolved about the prewar times and onwards and stressed that the in- and out-group conflicts were experienced more strongly than ever before. Their families come from Bosniac ethnic background and they used to be influential in the city. In such a small community people are very familiar with each other throughout their lives. This certainly brings lots of benefits but also lots of obstacles due to high expectations. The two sisters from these three families unveiled their examples of exclusion from their Bosniac ethnic group, simply because of their lower economic status:

> I hate the politics [...]. I hate this entire story about war and ethnicity. Here is all about the money!! Look at us! Our father was a very well-known man and while he was alive we enjoyed a good status in this city. Now, we are both single mothers and we are not able to find the simplest jobs [one of them with university degree and another secondary education]. The current mayor of the city is actually one of our first neighbours and our families were the best friends once. Our father had done so much for them [...], and now, not that they rejected helping us, they even stopped saying hello on the street. It is such a shame what people become just because of the money.

At the same time, for the members of the leading Bosniac families, the previous narrative and other similar ones, are simply result of a lack of people's political engagement and increased envy, which is characteristic for a small place such as Bugojno. In a rather short talk with a 51-year-old Bosniac nonmigrant and member of these ruling families this was confirmed:

> Here all people think that it is enough just to know you […], not to put any effort for work or other societal engagements [by "societal" he indirectly refers to political parties].

That subjective perception about civil society engagements might not be relevant for various in-group humanitarian events. The religious and diaspora networks have been active for the most vulnerable individuals and the floods in 2014 had overcome any possible divisions. The statements of the majority of people interviewed in Bugojno confirmed how important solidarity came to be across the city in that period. A 45-year-old male Bosniac nonmigrant relates his story:

> The times of floods were really exceptional for people's engagement with society. Not only were we collecting food, clothes and other available things, but we were also physically visiting places where the help was needed. My boss actually offered his trucks to deliver the help to Doboj [one of the most flood-affected cities]. I was personally driving several of these trucks. It was very hard but it was something special to all of us. The only important thing was to help.

Similar stories to those of the IDPs and nonmigrants were shared among the external BiH migrants in Bugojno. They all agreed that floods were an important moment to see how their society might become better rather than as it is. The ethnic division might be less important, or important in different way, as a 53-year-old Croat female returnee stated:

> I still believe that there is potential in this society to bring the ethnic diversity as benefit for all. We could learn so much from each other and also use our connections around the world in the best ways [she refers here to diaspora communities] as it was in the flood in 2014. We were all together in that situation. Everyone was communicating with everyone. I wish that time forever in this city. We are so small city and if we just do something small for others every day, we don't need any help form outside.

However, she and other BiH external migrants agree that several ruling families practically owned the city and that everything was still under their control. That made already existing ethnic tensions higher as people looked for any possibilities to resolve their housing and employment issues. A 56-year-old male external BiH migrant presented his life story as one of many in his surroundings. He came back to Bugojno after years of exile and now he lived there with his family. His wife worked in a shop and his children were students, while they still lived in a rented apartment. He had found his job through external BiH migrant networks from a neighbouring city:

> I was struggling for several years here with the job. I was working all that was on offer but it was hard to feed the family. My wife was also struggling to find work and she still works in a small supermarket, which is not her dream job for sure […]. But at least we are now more secure because I have a job in another city. I'm actually a truck driver for one Croat man while I'm a Bosniac. A friend of mine from Bugojno recommended me and that's how I've found this job. You can't say that all people are the same and I can give many examples as mine is […]. Yes, this city became all about division, ethnicity, money, and politics.

Novi Sad (Serbia)

Novi Sad is the second largest city in Serbia and capital of province of Vojvodina. Its population is about 300 000, of which the majority (90%) is Serbian, while the rest are Hungarian and then Slovak, Croat and other ethnic minorities. In addition to this multiethnic composition, there are many Bosnian Serb external migrants who settled in Novi Sad during the Bosnian war in 1990s. This was not the only movement of Bosnian Serbs moving to this city. The city has a long tradition of hosting the Serbian population from northern parts of Bosnia during the last century. The Serbs came to Novi Sad through several waves. They have all have been granted citizenship by the Republic of Serbia. However, that has little impact on their employment and housing status. Due to various administrative difficulties on the regional level, almost no institutional help to support the integration of refugee Serbs in this city was provided. That might be partly explained by the economic and political unrest in the country followed by painful transition processes. Within these circumstances, the reception of the BiH migrants groups, despite their same ethnic background, have not been as expected. In the most cases, the BiH external migrants were left on their own, which created strong ties between them but also weaker ties with the rest of the society. They are still labelled as "Bosnians" or "refugees" despite their full participation in the city for more than 20 years. Moreover, depending on their economic status they are still settled in the semiurban and less developed areas of Novi Sad. They have built the neighbourhoods or filled the neighbourhoods that were about to disappear demographically. That is the case for mostly working-class BiH external migrants, while those with better economic positions have settled around the city centre. Many of those with high education are employed in the municipal institutions or the private sector, such as in banks and international corporations, or they are running their own businesses. For those with the lower qualifications, the public employment is frequently replaced by self-employment in the markets, in small shops, as street sellers, as taxi drivers, or as workers in local firms (run mostly by other Bosnians). There is hardly any diasporic organization, with the exception of the latest proposed political party movement of the Serbs from ex-Yugoslav republics. The goal of this party is the political empowerment of individuals and the BiH external migrant group in Novi Sad.

Within this framework, informal networking was the strongest feature of the social capital of BiH external migrants in Novi Sad. In-group ties replaced the absence of trust in institutions and people at national and local level. Ethnicity is, however, still important in the homogeneous ethnic environment. Indeed, in the interviews ethnicity was certainly an important aspect of the BiH external migrants' identity. The war experiences, in particular, made it even stronger than before. Many explain that the exile period made them explore their religion and become believers. To that regard, they perceived their presence in the ethnic majority society as highly appreciated. However, the feelings of belonging to the majority ethnic group has little influence on their livelihoods in Novi Sad. Ethnicity, for them, is therefore more about identity formation than any economic privileges. Their migrant status (refugee) and local belonging (in BiH) form their in-group ties, rather than ethnicity. In-group relationships still suffer from the inequalities deriving from other socioeconomic elements, although this is less so than in the case of homogenous societies in BiH. Those with higher economic status and education frequently form small in-groups networks, which are not always available to all BiH external migrants. However, they maintain strong solidarity and reciprocity among themselves and their employment and housing are the best examples of that. Many have found employment and built their houses through their diasporic networks. At the same time, the lack of their full participation in the municipal life is reflected in their attitudes to volunteering and other civic engagements outside their own group. The exception is the periods of floods in 2014, when they fully supported the populations affected by floods both in BiH and Serbia. These observations are demonstrated by several stories presented below.

The BiH external migrants share much in common due to their migrant status and limited contact with the mainstream society in Novi Sad. However, their experiences might be different due to their education and employment status. That appeared to be the case in all of the interviews and an example is given by interviews with a group of four BiH external migrants in Novi Sad. Two of them are a couple and others are their friends, who have the same origin in BiH. However, they have different educational backgrounds and employment status. In other words, they see their BiH and ethnic origin as the core of their lives but educational background certainly makes their integration in Novi Sad different. For example, a 46-year-old male BiH external migrant has a secondary education and works at the gas station. He obtained employment through informal BiH networks and he spends all his time with his compatriots. However, he feels isolated from the nonmigrant population in Novi Sad and from the BiH external migrants with high education and better status:

> I spend all my time with by Bosnians here, just with Bosnians. I don't have any friends from Novi Sad. This is actually my fifth job and I've found all of them thanks to "my people" (here he refers to BiH external migrants) […]. But we are all working class and we deal with the private sector only. You work for businesses people and most of them are again from BiH […]. I personally prefer to work for BiH businessmen because most of the workers are from Bosnia as well. It is best to be among your own people […]. Well, yes there is a gap with those with higher education. They have their own circles and also another "way of life."

In the same interview, the two women with higher education (one trained in medicine and another an economist) confirm this story. They found that it was much easier to integrate into society due to their educational background. A 46-year-old medical doctor managed to obtain employment in the most recognized public hospital in Novi Sad thanks to her profession. However, she still sees BiH as the core of her life, but in a different way from before:

I didn't know anything about the religion before I came here. After all that happened I started to discover "who I'm really" and my identity [she refers here to religion]. That makes my life easier, I think. It was not easy here and still it is not. But this is now the only home we have. That's why I prefer to organize my private life with people from Bosnia. We somehow share the same life struggles and stories. Although I have to admit that I was very lucky to settle in this city in a better way than many others. I should probably thank to my profession and also good people I came across. Many of them were from Novi Sad, so I can't say anything bad about the society.

Her story was confirmed by many other BiH external migrants, who secured their employment in some of the more reputable institutions or the service sector. At the same time, the stories of those with lower education background still confirm that BiH networks are crucial for their living and job environments. A couple in their fifties tell the story of many of the BiH external migrants by sharing their story:

We came here because of some relatives. But all support finished quickly and you have to take your responsibility for your own life. I was working as a driver for a number of Bosnian private firms. It was always working illegally and I decided after more than ten years and after some health problems emerged to do something for myself and my family. My wife also decided to join me (she didn't work before that) and now we are running a small business with vegetables and fruits at a local market. It is not easy to get up every morning at 5 a.m. and be here in all weather conditions. But, at least we are managing our lives and provide an education for our children. We have built our new home in a semiurban neighbourhood, where only BiH external migrants live. That is actually the best part of our life because the relationships in the neighbourhoods are great. Just now it is too much work and less time for social life. But we are for each other whenever is needed. You can simply rely on people there because we are all "refugees from Bosnia".

Hence, it should not be surprising that not only in this neighbourhood but also among other BiH external migrant networks in Novi Sad, the highest civic engagement has been achieved during the floods in 2014. People participated in various activities organized around the city. They also initiated a lot of activities to support not only the victims of floods in Serbia but also in BiH. According to 39-year-old female BiH external migrant, volunteering in the floods 2014 was also an obligation to all people, who have found themselves in the same situation as they were back in the times of war in BiH:

I was volunteering in several places at the times of floods in 2014. I was also visiting places here in Serbia to help people. It was important to help. When you know what is the pain and suffer to stay without home and everything just over the night, than the only thing you care is human being. It doesn't matter who they are and where you belong.

Plaški (Croatia)

Plaški is the fourth case study in this research and it shows how BiH external migrants have managed their livelihoods in a small semiurban environment in Croatia. The municipality of Plaški counts around 2000 people of whom the majority are BiH external migrants, mainly with Croat ethnic origin (just a few are ethnic Bosniacs). The population is therefore almost 100% of Croat ethnic origin with just a few Serb returnees. That structure changed in comparison to prewar times, when a high percentage of populations was Serbian. Since majority never returned to Plaški and due to the housing policies in Croatia, majority of their houses and wealth was granted to new BiH external migrants arriving in the municipality. That is how their housing problem was resolved but not employment. Most BiH external migrants live on state aid as there are hardly any jobs in the municipality. The economy of the municipality relies on a few family businesses in agriculture, such as production of milk, cheese, honey and strawberries (the Municipality of Plaški) and the rest are either employed in the neighbouring cities or in seasonal jobs. The population is very religious and life in municipality is very much organized around the religious calendar and events. Mainly for that reason, the majority of BiH external migrants do not take ethnicity or their migrant (refugee) status into consideration. They were all granted Croatian citizenship and most are politically active in their municipality. Actually, the main division among them appears to be due the political orientation. They consider their political engagement important as it has provided them with the opportunity to negotiate the issues around their housing and monthly income (state aid), which makes their livelihoods in this municipality possible.

Ethnicity seems not be an important feature of the social capital in this small homogeneous municipality. The majority of BiH external migrants have strong trust in the local institutions and people, while they see the national level as more distance and beyond their influence. The informal and formal social networks among them are fairly strong. They are very much connected to each other and their informal networks are core of their daily lives. The formal organizations are mainly linked to religion (the Catholic Church). In both cases, not many of them reported difficulties in their work. The reason for that might be in their similar education and employment status. Most of them have secondary education and live on the state aid. For the rest, self-employment and small businesses, mainly in the agricultural field, are among the only available solutions. In such circumstances, it should be expected that there is a high level of collective action in the community. That, however, is not much of the case as the civic engagement of the BiH external migrants is very much connected to their political orientation. The exceptions, again, were seen in the time of the floods in BiH in 2014, when the majority helped or hosted their families from BiH. No collective activities towards help to rest of the population in BiH were organized. Collective action largely remains at the neighbourhood or friendship levels, while political activism makes them participate in important decision-making processes in their municipality. Some of their stories, described below, demonstrate how these dimensions of social capital and BiH external migrants in Plaški work on the ground.

The majority of BiH external migrants arrived in Plaški more by coincidence than due to any previous relationships to this small town. The majority had actually never been in touch with this municipality before their arrival in the 1990s. For example, a 55-year-old BiH external migrant arrived in Plaški with her son and father. She now owns a house and she still doesn't work but she inherited the pension from her father, who passed away in the meantime. Her son works in the wood industry and he is now planning to move to Zagreb for his work. She is satisfied with her life in Plaški because of her friends and neighbours but also because she feels like full member of this municipality:

> Well, I don't see that here ethnicity means something. We all go along very well with all of that. There are just a few prewar Serbian returnees and we also have a great relationships with them. The communication in the municipality is fine. People help each other and spend time with each other. I think that our main concern is about political orientation. I'm more left, for example, and if someone is more right oriented then we can have some disputes. But that's not something big. We are all engaged in the local political life and local elections are a central part of our lives. You know, you have to think how to resolve your own problems, especially when they were granting houses and other things. I managed thanks to my political engagement. It's easy here – everyone knows everyone. I honestly think the main problem here is high unemployment. Nothing has changed since the time of my arrival [...]. All the time we are just in this office for unemployment and all they offer to us are either some seasonal jobs in the

> EU (such as strawberry picking) or some physical jobs in the municipality or closer places (such as cleaning). That is not something you can do all your life and my son now needs to move to Zagreb to have a more secure future.

The difficult economic situation in the municipality was confirmed by one of the few Serbian returnee families. A Serbian couple in their late 60s returned to Plaški after many years of exile in Serbia. Their children and their families also returned with them. The reason for their return was nostalgia for Plaški and also lack of good opportunities in Serbia. They are both engineers, who worked in the large industrial centres in this area before the war. However, the previous economic system was destroyed during the war and they were forced to change to agriculture and set up a small family business. They are producing honey and their son runs a local bar. Meanwhile, this 68-year-old female of ethnic minority background in the Croat municipality was the mayor of the municipality for four years:

> Well, I thought that I should do something for this place and I also needed a job! The majority of people here only have lower education, so I thought I'd use my education and experience as well as my minority status [as a Serbian returnee] and do something for my family. The politics here is the only way forward. That's how it all started. I managed to become the mayor and during that period we also managed to resolve some of our main problems [...]. I can't complain about the people here but this is not nearly the society it used to be. The new population has nothing to do with the old one [...]. For me and my husband that is not important anymore, we would like to spend our time here but I really hope that my children will leave this place.

The good relationships in the neighbourhood were confirmed in all the other interviews. Despite the lack of employment opportunities, these people have found the new environment and way of living environment better than others in the region. This is also true of the older population due to the good institutional environment and better state care for their refugee problems. This could be observed through their civic participation in the municipality and how they saw themselves as a part of it. A 42-year-old male BiH external migrant explained how that operates for many of them:

> Well, we are all politically active here. I think that is very important. I can't say that there are no tensions in the political party. But there are still benefits as well. At least you can participate in the politics of the local municipality and try to make things better [...]. Of course, these personal reasons are also important [...]. In general, religion here is very important and we don't question ethnicity or ethnic belonging.

I think it is very clear what that means to us [he refers to religion]. Since we actually don't even bring that into the question, probably, we are more focused only on our role in the local life of the municipality itself.

This and other interviews further clarify that, in this small municipality, life is organized around weekly gatherings in the churches, where even political disputes disappear. For them, the solidarity and reciprocity that have emerged in these common religious events make their lives easier and more comfortable. However, a lack of economic opportunities is the main reason for more involvement in broader social action, including providing assistance during the floods in 2014.

Conclusion

Despite ethnic unmixing during the 1990s wars and forced displacement, ethnic diversity still remains an important factor affecting social capital in the postwar SEE environment. The case studies presented in this chapter confirm that and confirm what has been described in the existing literature, focused primarily on BiH (UNDP, 2009; Popova, 2009; Petrovic, 2007). The four case studies demonstrate that no general statements linking ethnicity to the three main dimensions of social capital are possible. In contrast, different political and economic environments, along with individual socioeconomic characteristics and migrant status, still influence social capital in both ethnically homogenous or heterogeneous social environments. The relationships between minorities and the majority, between and within three ethnic groups in the homogenous and heterogeneous ethnic communities, are experienced differently on the ground. The examples of homogenous communities show the importance of ethnicity for social capital but, along with migrant status, the most important factors include the level of education, employment status, economic performance and other socioeconomic characteristics including gender. Among all the three groups, individuals with a higher education and with an adequate employment status are frequently less sensitive to the issues of ethnicity, unless this is directly relevant to their individual material needs. At the same time, in these heterogeneous postwar environments, all aspects of everyday life are organized around ethnicity, both in public and private spheres. In those circumstances, social capital depends largely on the family and personal connections. As confirmed by UNDP (2009), even migrant status has less influence than it might be expected.

Hence, in-group relationships for both majority and minority ethnic groups in homogenous and heterogeneous communities are largely based on the intersection between ethnicity and other shared socioeconomic characteristics. This frequently leads to the exclusionary side of the social capital (Bourdieu, 1986; Portes, 1998; Gauntlet, 2011), where an ethnic group is further influenced by the power relations and social inequality. However, exclusionary social capital might also produce the opposite effect when, for instance, members of different ethnic groups join forces to resolve their employment problems or improve living conditions, as already confirmed by other researchers in BiH (see Efendic *et al.*, 2015). For many migrants, the local areas to which they belonged before migration or everyday neighbourhood engagements might remain more important than broader identity categories and those created through forced ethnic divisions (Čapo and Halilovich, 2013). Moreover, in-group relationships, to certain extent, might be overcome by a better political and economic environment, as in the case from Croatia (Plaški). With political and civic participation in their local municipalities, the migrant populations from the same or different ethnic groups might improve their positions and overcome ethnic tensions, although this is still largely failing to happen in BiH (Porobic and Memeledzija, 2013).

Finally, the in-group struggles identified here might lead to better "out-group" relationships. Although, collaboration among the members of different ethnic groups might not always lead to certain accumulation of social capital, it still might significantly improve everyday life in multiethnic communities. This has been proved to be the case in all four case studies and the stories from the field: members of different ethnic groups join their forces wherever there is an opportunity to gain a certain economic or other shared benefits. The examples of cooperation between women from different ethnic backgrounds or with different migrant status show that solidarity and reciprocity beyond ethnicity and religion still exist in this region. This and a number other positive examples should therefore gain more attention in further research. Moreover, particular attention should be devoted to the examples of collective action organized around the floods in the region, in 2014. Without exception, the four case studies showed that volunteering, donating, empathy and other forms of prosocial behaviour are still alive in the postwar environment in the times of crises. Despite the fact that the relationships between trust and (in)formal networking are changeable and not always positive, people's willingness to join forces in collective action in the most difficult circumstances certainly deserves detailed investigation and understanding. This would broaden our knowledge on how social capital might be built up from below and integrated in the often structurally and ethnically divided postwar environments in the SEE region.

ADNAN EFENDIC

Ethnic Diversity and Economic Performance of Individuals and Households in a Postconflict Environment – Evidence from Bosnia and Herzegovina

Introduction

Efendic *et al.* (2015) found that ethnic diversity in the postconflict environment of Bosnia and Herzegovina (BiH) is beneficial for young businesses. Young companies (entrepreneurs) in local areas that are ethnically diverse have systematically higher growth aspirations in comparison with ethnically homogenous areas. These results are important when seen in the context of the cross-country economic literature, as the latter suggests that ethnic heterogeneity may be associated with negative economic outcomes (e.g. Easterly and Levine, 1997; Collier, 1998; Easterly, 2001; Patsiurko *et al.*, 2012). Motivated by this research and a growing body of literature that investigates the effect of ethnic diversity in economics (also presented in Chapter 2), we conducted a new survey in the household sector of BiH to investigate whether ethnic diversity of the neighbouring area is associated with individual and household economic performance. While the existing literature primarily explores, directly or indirectly, diversity caused by immigration, our sample is uniquely different. We investigate a country that has been ethnically diverse over centuries and is, hence, an authentically diverse area. Two decades ago, this ethnically heterogeneous composition changed as a result of the Bosnian war (1992–1995). The economic consequences of the subsequent change towards ethnic homogeneity in some areas on individuals and families remains unknown.

In the first section of this chapter we provide a short background on the postconflict context of Bosnia and Herzegovina, in which we address why this country is appropriate for such an investigation. A discussion of the relevant literature is covered in the following section, then we continue by discussing the survey design and the data collected for this study including a discussion of the key variables of interest – those measuring individual economic performance and ethnic diversity. "Model specification and descriptive statistics" explains how theoretical concepts and models are matched to variables derived from survey questions and empirical models for estimation. This section also provides descriptive statistics about the variables used in empirical modelling. In our penultimate section we report the empirical findings and relevant statistical tests and discuss the key results. We conclude by summarizing key empirical findings and providing the main policy implications from this study.

The Postconflict Context of BiH

To investigate the research question of interest – whether ethnic diversity is associated with individual and household economic performance – we focus on Bosnia and Herzegovina, a postconflict transition country, which is a particularly appropriate context for such a study. Throughout its one thousand-years-long history, BiH had been recognized as a multicultural environment, mixing Eastern and Western cultural and religious influences. Even today, BiH is a multicultural country with one of the most "complicated" ethnic structures in Europe.

When BiH was part of former Yugoslavia (1945–1992), it was the country (i.e. the former Yugoslav republic) particularly well known for its multiethnic, multicultural, multireligious environment and the country with the highest level of ethnic tolerance among other Yugoslav republics (Hodson *et al.*, 1994; Efendic, 2010; Dyrstad, 2012). Unfortunately, the Bosnian war (1992–1995), which followed the dissolution of former Yugoslavia, caused a structural break for the ethnic composition within the country; namely, a change from ethnic diversity to ethnic homogeneity in many of its previously heterogeneous areas. This was also the period when a multiethnic BiH went through a structural change from ethnically quite tolerant to quite intolerant in just a few years (Dyrstad, 2012). Two decades after the Bosnian war, the country still remains highly segregated along ethnic lines, where the three main ethnic groups (Bosniacs, Serbs and Croats) have substantial autonomy and control over their own ethnoterritorial units (Bieber, 2010). Despite all these changes, there are regions within the country in which ethnic diversity is still preserved and this applies especially to microunits, such as municipalities and neighbourhoods. Accordingly, variations in ethnic diversity between different areas – in particular, at the level of microunits – constitute a fertile terrain for investigating the potential influence of ethnic homogeneity/diversity on the economic performance of individuals and household living in these areas. These alternative perspectives remain unexplored in the literature, especially in the context of the Western Balkan region.

Why it is relevant to investigate the effect of ethnic diversity at individual and household level in Bosnia and Herzegovina? First, the literature review presented in Chapter 2 informs us that the effect of ethnic diversity might be different at different levels of analysis. There are already a good number of macro and mesoeconomic focused studies but this is the first research, to the best of our knowledge, which investigates a direct effect of diversity on individual and household income, thus, bringing a novel focus to the existing literature. Second, individual and household strategies are affected by ethnic diversity even in situations where they have no preference for or against homogeneity. For example, depending on the areas where they live, individuals might establish their personal networks as ethnically homogenous or heterogeneous, which, in turn, could lead to different economic consequences discussed previously. Third, we can list two statistical arguments for this investigation as well. There is much more variation in ethnic diversity data at micro levels (e.g. neighbourhoods, cities) than at higher levels of analysis (regional or country level investigations). For example, while different regions and entities in BiH are often ethnically homogeneous, on average, a number of municipalities, cities, local communities and neighbourhoods within these regions are still ethnically diverse. In addition, a micro-level specification with diversity data is less likely to suffer from endogeneity bias compared to macro and growth specifications, where the literature has already identified a number of indirect influences of ethnic diversity that should be taken into account. Finally, this research has policy implications that are important for this and similar postethnic conflict environments.

Ethnic Diversity and Economic Performance Literature

As we pointed out in Chapter 2, the literature shows the importance of ethnicity for different economic outcomes, while we can identify studies supporting the opposite hypothesis – ethnic diversity is found to have both positive and negative effect on economic performance. A number of empirical studies report a negative effect of ethnic diversity on economic outcomes. Easterly and Levine (1997) focus on ethnolinguistic diversity at the national level and find that ethnic diversity is associated with slow economic growth in Africa. Moreover, the effect of ethnic diversity is not only negative in its direct effect on economic growth; ethnic diversity partly explains variations in economically relevant indirect indicators such as schooling, political stability, financial systems, foreign exchange markets, government consumption and infrastructure. From this point of view, ethnic diversity can exert indirect effects by influencing the operation of channels or policies that affect long-run growth rates. In this vein, Escaleras and Register (2011) find that ethnic diversity and tensions negatively affect the formation of social infrastructure (e.g., public utilities, education, health care), thereby imposing an unnecessary burden on growth and development. Similarly, Alesina *et al.* (1999) investigate a sample of US cities and find that greater ethnic diversity in US local jurisdictions is associated with higher spending and higher deficits/debt *per capita*, but still with lower provision of core public goods like education and roads.

Collier (1998) in a cross-sectional study of the effect of ethnic diversity on economic growth finds that maximally diverse societies grow more slowly than do homogenous societies. However, he also finds that diversity is damaging to growth primarily in the context of limited political rights, while this effect is not clearly identified in democratic societies. Easterly (2001) also identifies the negative effect of diversity on economic growth, but the authors report that it is not an isolated effect and might be mitigated by good institutions. In line with this, Goren (2014) identifies a direct negative effect of ethnic diversity on economic growth in a global sample as well as number of indirect transmission channels through which diversity may affect growth – namely, schooling, political instability, market distortions, trade openness and fertility rate. Patsiurko *et al.* (2012), however, also report a negative association between ethnic fractionalization and economic growth for OECD economies. The authors identify the greater importance of "ethnic fractionalization" in comparison to other forms of fractionalizations, such as religious and linguistic. Similarly, Montalvo and Reynal-Querol (2005), in their cross-country research, likewise find that ethnic polarization has a negative effect on economic development. These authors argue that ethnic polarization reduces investment, increases government consumption and entails a higher probability of civil conflict, which, ultimately, reduces economic development. Although the literature discussed above identifies a negative effect of ethnic diversity on economic performance, the perspective of these studies is primarily macroeconomic and is often focused on indirect influences on economic outcomes (e.g. through its effect on government efficiency and provision of public goods and services).

There is also a growing body of literature that finds a positive effect of ethnic diversity on economic performance. Alesina and La Ferrara (2005) argue that more diverse groups with limited abilities can perform better than more homogenous groups of high-ability problem solvers. Hence, individuals involved in more diverse groups, networks and environments can find better solutions to difficult problems and so become economically more productive. The same authors develop a theoretical framework in which the skills of individuals from different ethnic groups are complementary in the process of production, which in turn increases productivity. Based on this framework, the authors conduct an empirical investigation using US data and find that greater ethnic diversity is associated with higher income level of the community under study. Similarly, Jacobs (1961) sees ethnic diversity as the key factor of success of a city and as an engine of urban development. Ottaviano and Peri (2006) find that ethnic diversity is associated with higher wages of the resident population in US cities, hence, producing a positive effect on the economic performance of individuals. Bellini *et al.* (2013) conduct similar research, focusing on European regions in 12 EU countries. They find consistent results – namely, ethnic diversity is positively correlated with productivity, where causation goes from diversity to productivity.

We can consider not only the issue of whether ethnic diversity affects economic performance but also which type of diversity is considered. For example, Collier (2001) categorizes ethnic diversity into "dominance" and "fractionalization". The authors find that ethnically diverse societies characterized by ethnic dominance are likely to have worse economic performance, while in diverse societies characterized by ethnic fractionalization this is not necessarily the case, especially in democratic societies. In other words, ethnic diversity is damaging if it takes the form of dominance over fractionalization.

Unlike the previous sample of studies, the literature that reports a positive effect of ethnic diversity is more meso-micro oriented and focused on regions, cities and individuals. Indeed, the effects of ethnic diversity might be different at different levels of economic analysis (Alesina and La Ferrara, 2005), especially because macro studies need to take into account a number of indirect influences on economic outcomes (Goren, 2014). Nevertheless, as indicated earlier, we aim to investigate the effect of ethnic diversity on economic performance within a specific postconflict society[1] and at individual/household level. There is much more variation in the data at microlevel and for that reason this focus provides a promising strategy for the investigation that follows.

The Survey Design and Variables of Interest

In this analysis, we investigate public opinion from the household sector obtained through a cross-sectional survey conducted in BiH by a professional agency. This survey was conducted over the period June–October 2012.[2] The interviews were face-to-face meetings based on Computer-Assisted Personal Interviewing (CAPI) methodology, which resulted in no missing observations.[3]

---

1   In the literature reviewed above, many authors (e.g. Alesina and La Ferrara, 2005) distinguish ethnic from linguistic and religious groups in their research and analyse these differences separately. In the context of BiH, however, there are no "real" language differences inside the country between different ethnicities. In contrast, the dominant ethnicities in BiH (Bosniacs, Serbs, and Croats) largely correspond to religious differentiations (Muslims, Orthodox and Catholics respectively).

2   The survey questions were piloted by the researcher in seven cities (40 individuals) in May 2012. The sample covered both entities and three dominant ethnicities where each ethnicity was the majority in two cities. After piloting, relevant modifications were made to the questions.

3   Computer-Assisted Personal Interviewing is face-to-face interviewing based on computer technology used to administer the questionnaire. According to Foster and McCleery (1999), a major advantage of CAPI is that it reduces respondent error.

Although this is a household survey, we dealt with the individual responses (only one individual per household) of adults who are citizens of BiH. Each individual was randomly selected for interview based on the sample criteria. The targeted sample was 2000 individuals (effectively, we dealt with 2017 observations) and was designed to be representative of two entities in BiH (Federation of BiH and Republika Srpska), regions (16 regions), municipalities (141), ethnic groups (Bosniacs, Serbs and Croats), genders and urban/rural areas. A unique feature of this dataset is that it was designed to capture information on ethnic diversity and economic performance at the individual and household level.

Although the survey dataset has no missing values, "don't know" or, for some questions, "don't wish to answer" responses accounted on average for 3.5% of responses, while around 7% of the sample responded in this way to the questions on personal income and ethnic minority/majority status. In surveys, "don't know" or "don't wish to answer" responses are typically relatively high for income and ethnicity variables. Nonetheless, in this survey, the incidence of these responses to the questions of interest is either below or not much higher than 5% (see Table 6.1). In the imputation literature, this is the level of missing values at which simple "listwise deletion" – i.e. omission – is regarded as unlikely to lead to substantial bias, even when the missing values are not necessarily "missing at random".

The second challenge when attempting to make a valid estimation with survey data is to take account of survey design. The survey design for this sample is straightforward: the whole of BiH was stratified into 16 regions (10 covering the Federation of BiH, five the Republika Srpska and one the District of Brcko); then individuals were sampled within each stratum (region). In our case, no finite population correction (FPC) was made. This simple survey design makes almost no difference to estimation; stratification leads to a tiny increase in precision, but in no case is it sufficient to make a difference to whether or not estimates are reported with statistical significance. The disadvantage of this simple design is that it makes no allowance for possible clustering effects in the data. Consequently, in estimating our model we:

Routing errors are eliminated because the script automatically routes to the correct questions. In addition, it ensures that data are generally more complete, can considerably reduce the number of "nonresponses" and, correspondingly, the need for corrective editing.

- ignore the stratification, but instead
- report cluster-robust standard errors to allow for arbitrary patterns of correlation at the level of the 128 municipalities covered by the sample (from 141, some of which have a population as small as a few hundred) and
- include a full set of regional dummies, with Sarajevo as the reference category.

This estimation strategy minimizes the possibility of omitted variables related to location and adopts a conservative approach to inference.

The dependent variable that we used in our modelling procedure is the economic performance of individuals and families, which we proxy by the total monthly income of respondents. Bosnia and Herzegovina is a country with huge official unemployment (around 30%) and, correspondingly, a substantial amount of income is earned in the grey economy, which is estimated to be around 30% of total economic activity. (We obtained a similar percentage of informally employed in our sample.) Accordingly, in order to capture the economic performance of individuals better, we asked participants to report their total monthly income from whatever source and provided them with a scale of different income categories. The scale had previously been tested and designed by the professional research agency based on previous surveys conducted in this country. We believe that this is a better strategy for investigating the total income of individuals than relying on official indicators, which overestimate the unobserved economy. While some of the existing research uses official indicators to proxy the productivity of individuals in the ethnic diversity literature (e.g. Ottaviano and Pery, 2006; Bellini et al., 2013) our approach, which includes earnings from the informal economy, is more suitable for this particular sample.

Measuring ethnic diversity is not a straightforward task and it seems that researchers are still searching for appropriate measures or indicators of ethnicity and diversity. Generally, ethnicity and ethnic groups are slippery concepts (Fearon, 2003) and far from straightforward (Posner, 2000). Posner (2000), Constant and Zimmermann (2009) and Efendic *et al.* (2011) use different measures of ethnic diversity obtained from survey data. The survey approach seems promising for our research, bearing in mind that ethnic perceptions are subjective and the product of self-definition (Posner, 2000). Accordingly, we followed a practice suggested by Fearon (2003) and asked respondents questions about their ethnic-self-identification and perceptions of the ethnic diversity of their neighbourhoods.

Our main research objective is to examine whether the economic performance of individuals and families, proxied by their total monthly income, is affected by the ethnic composition (diversity) of the areas in which they live. To obtain a proxy for the diversity variable, we simply asked respondents to describe the level of ethnic diversity in their neighbourhood. Following Efendic *et al.* (2015), we provided the range of possibilities (1–5) where (1) means that there is only one ethnicity in the neighbourhood and (5) means that the area is very diverse. This question had been already tested in this country and an empirical investigation was implemented based on that work.

We are also interested to capture ethnic status according to whether individuals perceive themselves as belonging to the minority or the majority ethnic group. Fearon (2003) reports that around 70% of countries in the world have an ethnic group that accounts for the absolute majority; however, that is not the case for BiH. In the context of BiH it is important to control for majority/minority status within the country not least because the three constituent ethnicities form majorities and minorities in different parts of the country. Accordingly, at the individual level, we can expect variations in economic variables depending on self-reported majority/minority status, which is often identified as important in empirical research (e.g. Efendic *et al.*, 2011; Vanhoutte and Hooghe, 2012). If there is some discrimination based on ethnic minority-majority status (e.g. minorities sometimes claim more problems in finding employment), this variable should capture that effect on total income.

After presenting the main variables of interest we continue with the model specification and introduce other controlled variables.

Model Specification and Descriptive Statistics

Our modelling strategy is guided by theory concerning potential links between ethnic diversity and the economic performance of individuals and households measured by the level of total monthly income. Our initial model is underpinned theoretically by the Mincer earning equation

(Mincer, 1974). The Mincer earning function is a single-equation model that explains earnings as a function of schooling and experience. The equation has been examined in many datasets and it remains one of the most widely used models in empirical economics (Lemieux, 2006), including a whole range of augmented models. Typically, the logarithm of earnings is modelled as the sum of years of education and a quadratic function of years of potential experience. This is our platform for augmentation with our variables of interest.

We estimate a personal income (Equation 6.1) model with the following baseline specification:

$$\ln earning_i = \beta_1 + \beta_2 \cdot age_i + \beta_3 \cdot age2_i + \beta_4 \cdot educat_i + \beta_5 \cdot d\_diversity_i$$
$$+ X \cdot \beta_K + \hat{u}_i \qquad (6.1)$$

In Equation (6.1) the dependent variable is *lnearning_i* and this denotes the respondent's level of personal income in logarithmic form; $_i$ is the index for cross-section observations. The Mincer equation coefficients to be estimated include β_1 as the intercept term; β_2 and β_3 are the coefficients to be estimated for variables capturing age (age_i) and squared age ($age2_i$) of respondents; β_4 estimates the effect of different levels of education (*education_i*) in the model; and $\hat{u}_i$ is the error term with standard characteristics.

The initial Mincer equation is augmented with the variable of interest, a dummy variable *d_diversity*. β_5 estimates the effect of ethnic diversity on personal income. Recall, this variable measures whether the respondents' area is ethnically homogenous (0) or diverse (1). We use a dummy variable because some 42% of the surveyed areas are reported to be ethnically homogenous.

Finally, we include a vector (*X*) of controlled variables that might be important influences on earnings, including: *d_majority* measuring self-identification of respondents as belonging to minority or majority ethnic group; *d_urban,* a dummy variable capturing whether the surveyed area is urban or rural (official indicators for BiH suggest that average earnings are generally higher in urban than rural areas); and *d_female* coding the gender of respondents (official sources also report that gross earnings of male respondents are higher than of female respondents). Finally, we include dummy variables for each surveyed region, but these are not reported (there are 16 regions; hence, 15 regional dummy variables are part of each estimated specification).

Descriptive statistics for the variables used in the model are reported in Table 6.1.

Table 6.1 Definitions, construction and descriptive statistics of variables.

Variables	Explanation of dummy variables (do not know/wish to answer responses excluded)	Number of obser- vations	Do not knows (%)	Mean
Dependent variables				
earning	Personal income: 1 = 0€; 2 = 0–50€; ...; 11-over 1500 €	1870	7.3	3.45
fearning	Family income: 1 = 0€; 2 = 0–50€; ...; 11-over 1500 €	1870	7.3	1.04
lnearning	Level of personal income: logarithmic transformation	1755	12.9	4.80
lnfearning	Level of family income: logarithmic transformation	1755	12.9	1.42
Mincer equation variables				
age	Age of respondents	2017	0.0	51.82
age2	Age of respondents squared	2017	0.0	2985.61
education	The level of education: 1 = no educa- tion; 2 = elementary; ....; 5 = under- graduate level; 6 = postgraduate level	2012	0.2	3.01
Variable of interest – diversity				
d_diversity	Ethnic diversity: 1 = diverse; 0 = homogenous	1975	2.1	0.58
Other controlled variables				
d_majority	Self-identification: 1 = majority; 0 = minority	1857	7.0	0.79
d_urban	Geographic area: 1 = urban or subur- ban; 0 = rural	2013	0.2	0.64
d_female	Gender: 1 = female; 0 = male	2017	0.0	0.51
d_married	Marital status: 1 = married; 0 = other	2010	0.3	0.64
Regional dummies				
unasana	Unskosanski region = 1; 0 = other regions	2017	0.0	0.08
posavina	Posavina region = 1; 0 = other regions	2017	0.0	0.01
tuzla	Tuzla region = 1; 0 = other regions	2017	0.0	0.13
zenica	Zenicko-dobojski region = 1; 0 = other regions	2017	0.0	0.09

Variables	Explanation of dummy variables (do not know/wish to answer responses excluded)	Number of observations	Do not knows (%)	Mean
podrinje	Podrinjski region = 1; 0 = other regions	2017	0.0	0.01
centralbih	Srednjebosanski region = 1; 0 = other regions	2017	0.0	0.06
herzegneret	Hercegovackoneretvanski region = 1; 0 = other regions	2017	0.0	0.06
weshterzeg	Zapadnohercegovacki region = 1; 0 = other regions	2017	0.0	0.02
sarajevo	Sarajevo region = 1; 0 = other regions	2017	0.0	0.13
canton10	Canton 10 region = 1; 0 = other regions	2017	0.0	0.02
banjaluka	Banja Luka region = 1; 0 = other regions	2017	0.0	0.17
doboj	Doboj region = 1; 0 = other regions	2017	0.0	0.07
bijeljina	Bijeljina region = 1; 0 = other regions	2017	0.0	0.06
easternrs	Eastern RS region = 1; 0 = other regions	2017	0.0	0.05
easternherzeg	Eastern Herzegovina RS region = 1; 0 = other regions	2017	0.0	0.02
brcko	Brcko region = 1; 0 = other regions	2017	0.0	0.03

Source: Authors' calculations using STATA 14 (STATA 14, StataCorp, Texas, United States).

The variable of particular interest is *d_diversity*, which controls for whether the neighbourhood area is more or less diverse. The ethnic diversity of the surveyed area can be assumed to be exogenous because the ethnic composition within BiH was primarily war-induced some two decades earlier. Accordingly, we specify a direct exogenous effect of ethnic diversity on economic performance of individuals and households. Based on findings by Efendic *et al.* (2015) and the general diversity literature (Jacobs, 1961; Miguel *et al.*, 2003; Ottaviano and Peri, 2006; Bellini *et al.*, 2013) we expect that ethnic diversity might have beneficial effects on individual economic performance measured through the estimated level of personal and family income. Accordingly, we state our main hypothesis:

Ethnic diversity in different areas of BiH is beneficial for economic performance – income – of individuals and their families.

Empirical Investigation

We estimate a single equation model by Ordinary Least Squares (OLS). Being concerned with heterogeneity of the data identified in our checking procedure, we estimate a cluster robust inference where surveyed municipalities are used as clusters. Before we present and interpret our findings, we check standard model diagnostics for functional form, multicollinearity and joint significance. The results of these tests are reported in Table 6.2; all the estimated models have appropriate model diagnostics.

Table 6.2 Results from the baseline OLS model (cluster-robust inference).

(Dependent variable: *lnearning*)								
	Mincer base specification Model (1)		**Mincer specification with diversity only Model (2)**		**Preferred diversity personal income Model (3)**		**Diversity family income Model (4)**	
Variable	**Coeff.**	**P> |t|**	**Coeff**	**P>|t|**	**Coeff.**	**P>|t|**	**Coeff**	**P>|t|**
Mincer's variables								
age	0.02	0.000	0.03	0.000	0.03	0.000	−0.01	0.005
age2	−0.01	0.001	−0.01	0.000	−0.01	0.000	0.01	0.067
education	0.22	0.000	0.18	0.000	0.19	0.000	0.15	0.000
Diversity variables								
d_diversity	–	–	0.09	0.018	0.09	0.025	0.08	0.008
Controlled variables								
d_urban	–	–	–	–	0.09	0.024	0.15	0.000
d_female	–	–	–	–	−0.17	0.000	0.01	0.706
d_majority	–	–	–	–	0.05	0.209	0.06	0.067
d_married	–	–	–	–	−0.09	0.012	0.08	0.011
Model diagnostics								
Number of observations	1865		1825		1713		1588	
R-squared	0.16		0.18		0.20		0.19	
Ramsey RESET test	Prob > F = 0.10		Prob > F = 0.16		Prob > F = 0.37		Prob > F = 0.07	
VIF	4.71		4.47		4.47		4.45	
The Wald	Prob > F = 0.00		Prob > F = 0.00		Prob > F = 0.00		Prob > F = 0.00	

Notes: Regional dummies included but not reported for reasons of space.

Source: Authors' calculations using STATA 14 (STATA 14, StataCorp, Texas, United States).

We found that all the variables in the initial Mincer equations (Models 1 and 3) are statistically significant and estimated with the expected sign. Education has the highest positive effect in the model, while experience has a positive effect but with a decreasing rate. After we augment the initial model with diversity and control variables, these "core" effects continue to appear with the same respective signs and similar magnitudes. This is an important robustness check for the initial model. Our preferred specification for individual earning function is Model 3; and for the family earnings function Model 4. We now interpret these results.

Level of education has the highest positive effect in the models. On average, there is a 19% higher income reported by educated individuals in comparison to those without education or with only primary education. A positive association between education and individual earnings confirms the importance of investment in education.

Experience of respondents affects earning as well. The older respondents report higher income. However, the relationship is not linear and it is subject to decreasing returns.

Ethnic diversity of the surveyed areas is a statistically significant and positive effect in both estimated models. Respondents living in more diverse areas, on average and holding all other factors constant, report 9% higher income in comparison to those individuals living in ethnically homogenous areas. This result is consistent with Efendic *et al.* (2015) who report a positive effect of ethnic diversity in the business sector of BiH economy. Accordingly, we do not have enough evidence to reject the stated hypothesis. The effect of ethnic diversity has an economically substantial effect that should not be ignored by policymakers. Moreover, this finding holds for family income as well (Model 4).

The gender of respondents is a significant influence on income, with women on average – and holding all other factors constant – reporting a 17% smaller income than men. This is consistent with official indicators that record lower earnings for women. However, the estimated effect of gender is higher than is suggested by official statistics, which is consistent with our strategy to capture the effect of the unobserved economy in earnings. Accordingly, this finding implies that there might be income inequality based on gender in the informal economy as well, which could be an important issue for further investigation.

The urban/rural area difference exerts quite an important effect in the model, suggesting that respondents and families living in urban areas reported higher incomes than those in urban areas.

Discussion of the Results

The literature review established that ethnic diversity might have positive or negative effects on economic performance and these differences mainly depend on the level of analysis. The majority of studies reporting a negative effect on economic outcomes are macro oriented and often identify different indirect influences on economic growth and development. A positive effect of ethnic diversity is more often reported at lower levels of economic analysis, such as regions, cities or individuals. Our investigation was micro-oriented, focused on individuals and their families. Our findings are consistent with most of the microfocused literature: ethnic diversity of neighbouring areas is not an economic threat but is rather associated with positive outcomes – higher incomes – for individuals and families.

Bosnia and Herzegovina has been a multicultural environment for more than 1000 years and our findings suggest that this authentic diversity is economically beneficial for its individuals and families. Our finding should be interpreted in the context of our sample, bearing in mind that ethnic diversity has often been investigated in the framework of ethnic heterogeneities caused by immigration and inflow of different cultures and traditions into homogenous areas. Conversely, shifts towards homogenization in much of BiH are something new, introduced by war with unknown consequences. This study emphasizes that policies favouring ethnic homogeneity, which are still propounded by some political forces in this still multicultural environment, are likely to cause medium-to-long-run welfare losses for BiH citizens. To sum up, ethnic diversity is of policy interest because it can be influenced by public authorities – for example return migration policy, which has rather failed in its goal.

We conclude that the evidence does not reject the stated hypothesis: ethnic diversity in the surrounding neighbourhood is associated positively with greater individual and household income.

Conclusion

We used unique cross-sectional survey data to investigate the effect of ethnic diversity on individual and household economic performance in Bosnia and Herzegovina. The complexity of their interrelationship in the context of this postconflict country is addressed and investigated by estimating models in which ethnic diversity directly affects personal and family incomes.

The last conflict in BiH (1992–1995) was ethnically characterized and harmful for ethnic heterogeneity of this society. Still, two decades later, where ethnic diversity has been preserved, this study identifies the positive economic consequences for individuals and households. We find that individuals in ethnically diverse areas systematically report 9% higher income in comparison to those in ethnically homogenous regions. Policies and initiatives supporting ethnic homogeneity over diversity – still present in this long lasting ethnically diverse society – are harmful for economic performance of individuals and households. A corollary is that policymakers in this postconflict country and in similar environments elsewhere should promote ethnic diversity and, across the broad range of public policies, take into consideration the negative effect of ethnic homogeneity. This finding and corresponding policy implication is consistent with previous research reporting that the business sector in BiH benefits from ethnically diverse surrounding neighbourhoods.

Adnan Efendic, Bojana Babic and Anna Rebmann

Rebuilding SEE Region Through Different Forms of Social Capital

Social capital – often defined as the goodwill that is created by the fabric of social relations and that can be mobilized to facilitate prosocial actions – is a crucial building block of societies. As such it is linked to institutional efficiency, economic development, reduced crime rates and a reduced incidence of other social problems and challenges. The core element of social capital, within its various conceptualizations (including the multidimensional one adopted in this research), remains relations among people, interactions and approaches to resources. Social capital can thus play an important role in everyday lives and postcrisis recovery by encouraging prosocial behaviour, by facilitating proactive participation by individuals and communities in recovery and rehabilitation activities and can serve as "informal insurance" during or after a crisis or disaster (Aldrich, 2010, 2012). With such a role, social capital remains of research and policy interest, especially for postconflict societies that are struggling in their socioeconomic reintegration and recovery, as is the case in southeast Europe (SEE).

This book confirms that social capital remains an important social building block in the reintegration processes of the selected SEE communities. Such a conclusion challenges the common belief that (re)establishing social relations in a postconflict environment is difficult, or sometimes even impossible. Our analysis implies that the sustainability of people's livelihoods is supported by different forms of social capital emerging on a daily basis within and between different population strata. However, these are also societies where trust in people and institutions remain low and are often replaced with other dimensions of social capital, where we identify the particular importance of informal networking among different groups. Different dimensions of social capital appear to be dynamic; they sometimes complement each other but also sometimes substitute the failures of some aspects of society. What we find is that when formal institutional solutions are failing in their goals, social capital was there to substitute for these gaps and this was done mainly through informal networking, prosocial behaviour, solidarity and empathy, in particular in the periods of crisis and postcrisis recovery on which we focused.

Internal and external migrants face often greater socioeconomic challenges than the nonmigrant population. In such circumstances, migrants consistently report that their everyday lives have been sustained due to established social relationships within their own "communities", "migrant networks" and "translocal neighbourhoods" (also identified in other literature such as Povrzanovic-Frykman, 2002; Kaya, 2009; Capo and Halilovich, 2013). A lot of blame is placed on formal institutions, which are perceived as ineffective, corrupt, useless and untrustworthy entities, while other forms of social capital are used to fill the gap created by inefficient institutional environments. Such socioeconomic realities have given rise to new structural dimensions of social capital – formal and informal networking of people – replacing and compensating for the lack of trust in institutions as well as the lack of economic and social opportunities, especially for the migrant population. We identify a large presence of informal networks in this society, often based on strong ties – mostly family based but also built around respondents' migration status, ethnicity, geography, or individual socioeconomic characteristics. Targeted and selective networking seems to be an efficient dimension of social capital, including internal and external migrants' "migrant networks", which, as explained earlier, play a substitutive function for formal institutional shortcomings.

The findings from the qualitative research acknowledged both the importance of social capital in a postconflict environment and its complicated performance for different categories. We also conducted an in-depth analysis of two periods relevant for social capital investigation – a crisis period (floods) and a noncrisis period – in order to consider better postconflict environment. This quantitative investigation of social capital activities and outcomes – i.e. prosocial behaviour – indicates that individual behaviours are joint outcomes of a wider system of observed and unobserved endogenous influences. More social activities in a noncrisis period are linked with more prosocial engagement in the period of crisis (in our case the 2014 floods) – they are positively correlated. This outcome strongly suggests that building social capital in a normal period or in everyday life is an investment in a more secure positive response of citizens when society is confronted with sudden challenges, crisis and hurdles. Again, this signifies the importance of building social capital as an investment in a better future and a socially more active and responsive society; it has the potential to overcome lack of economic resources, regardless of assistance from national and international agencies, and to reduce the level of damage, facilitating postcrisis recovery and reconstruction. However, this remains ignored when it comes to policymaking and at various structural levels (from local to national). For that reason, it is important to investigate social capital inputs more closely in different local environments.

The investigations also reveal that social capital outcomes are under a strong influence of different social capital inputs. In particular, membership in different societal groups and more networking of people – hence, structural social capital – explains more prosocial behaviour. In the context of network structure, the ethnic diversity of networks, which is particularly relevant in ethnically mixed societies, is beneficial for engagement in prosocial behaviour. Although the local levels are often considered through the lens of ethnicity, this has no or little influence on prosocial behaviour and interethnic collaboration in normal and crisis periods.

Inspired by the previous finding, we established a special focus on the role of ethnicity and ethnic self-identification in prosocial engagement of citizens in the whole SEE region. The qualitative investigation in Chapter 5 identified the relevance of ethnicity to social capital, although we do have indications that level of education, employment status and the economic performance of individuals and households are often more influential determinants of prosocial behaviour, including both ethnically homogenous and heterogeneous environments. The in-group relationships for both majority and minority ethnic groups and in both homogenous and heterogeneous communities are largely based on the intersection between ethnicity and socio-economic characteristics that has been identified in other research (e.g. Li *et al.*, 2005; Petrovic, 2007; Popova, 2009; UNDP, 2009). A general finding is that individuals with a higher level of education and with a stable employment status are frequently less sensitive to any issue linked to ethnicity and consequently less sensitive to the negative effects of ethnic exclusion on societal relations.

The results suggest that collaboration among the members of different ethnic groups might not always lead to the accumulation of social capital; still, it improves everyday lives in ethnically diverse communities. This proved to be the case in real life, reflected in the interviews: members of different ethnic groups often join forces where there is an opportunity to gain economic or other social benefits, putting interethnic challenges aside. The examples of cooperation between women from different ethnic background or different migrant status show that solidarity and reciprocity beyond ethnicity and religion still exist. This also signifies the importance of economic performance of individuals and families as determinants of social interactions in these postconflict societies.

The last conflict in BiH was ethnically characterized and harmful for the ethnic heterogeneity of that society, its social capital and economic performance. Despite all these changes, there are regions within the country in which ethnic diversity is still there – where ethnic diversity has been preserved and the positive economic consequences for individuals and households cannot be ignored. We find that individuals in ethnically diverse areas systematically report higher income in comparison to ethnically homogenous regions. The shift towards homogenization in much of BiH is something new and imposed or, to put it more precisely, introduced by the war and violence with unknown economic consequences. This study emphasizes that policies favouring ethnic homogeneity, which are still propounded by some political forces in this multicultural environment, are likely to cause medium to long-term welfare loss to BiH citizens. To sum up, ethnic diversity is of policy interest because it can be influenced by public authorities – migration policy being an example that has rather failed as a postwar public goal. Our recommendation is that policymakers in this postconflict country and in similar environments elsewhere should promote ethnic diversity across the broad range of public policies while taking into consideration the negative effects of imposed ethnic homogeneity.

Our results conclude with a general recommendation that policymaking should understand the importance and specifics of social capital in the SEE region and focus their attention on new opportunities for civic engagement and building social capital. In particular, the local level (community and neighbourhood) is identified as playing a crucial role in organizing people's lives, while personal sociocultural characteristics such as education, ethnicity, religion, class and socioeconomic status are also important in establishing and sustaining daily communications. Social capital has been used to support everyday life but this social multidimensional capital needs more investment from policymakers to support long-term benefits in these societies. What people built through natural and informal collaboration on the ground can sometimes be a good signal to formal institutions in these societies. The best example is informal collaboration and networking, which integrates interethnic solidarity among ordinary people, while formal institutions in these countries mainly fail in achieving this goal.

References

Adam, F. and Roncevic, B (2003) Social capital: recent debates and research trends. *Social Science Information* 42(2), 155–183.

Adams, R. H. (2006) *International Migration, Remittances, and the Brain Drain.* The World Bank Policy Research Working Paper: 3069. World Bank, Washington, DC.

Adler, P. S. and Kwon, S.-W. (2002) Social capital: prospects for a new concept. *Academy of Management Review* 27(1), 17–40.

Akee, R., (2010) Who leaves? Deciphering immigrant self-selection from a developing country. *Economic Development and Cultural Change* 58(2), 323–344.

Akerlof, G. A., and Kranton, R. (2010) *Identity economics: how identities shape our work, wages, and well-being.* Princeton 2010.

Aldrich, D. P. (2010) Fixing recovery: social capital in post-crisis resilience. *Journal of Homeland Security,* 6, 1–10.

Aldrich, D. P. (2012) *Building Resilience: Social Capital in Post-disaster Recovery.* University of Chicago Press, Chicago, IL.

Alesina, A., Hausmann, R., Hommes, R. and Stein, E. (1999) Budget institutions and fiscal performance in Latin America. *Journal of Development Economics* 59(2), 253–273.

Alesina, A. and La Ferrara, E. (2002) Who trusts others? *Journal of Public Economics* 85(2), 207–234.

Alesina, A. and La Ferrara, E., (2005) Ethnic diversity and economic performance. *Journal of Economic Literature* 43(3), 762–800.

Alexander, K. (1976) The value of an education. *Journal of Education Finance* 1(4), 429–467.

Alexander, M. (2007) Determinants of social capital: new evidence on religion, diversity and structural change. *British Journal of Political Science* 37(2), 368–377.

Armstrong, J. (1982) *Nations Before Nationalism.* University of North Carolina Press, Chapel Hill, NC.

162

Bahna, M. (2008) Predictions of migration from the new member states after their accession into the European Union: successes and failures. *International Migration Review* 42(4), 844–860.

Baker, W. and Faulkner, R. R. (2009) Social capital, double embeddedness, and mechanisms of stability and change. *American Behavioral Scientist* 52(11), 1531–1555.

Beine, M., Docquier, F. and Rapoport, H. (2001) Brain drain and economic growth: theory and evidence. *Journal of Development Economics* 64(1), 275–289.

Bellini, E., Ottaviano, G. I., Pinelli, D. and Prarolo, G. (2013) Cultural diversity and economic performance: evidence from European regions. In *Geography, Institutions and Regional Economic Performance* (eds. R. Crescenzi and M. Percoco). Springer Berlin Heidelberg, Berlin, pp. 121–141.

Bieber, F. (2010) Executive power-sharing. In *Political Participation of Minorities. A Commentary on International Standards and Practice* (eds. M. Weller and K. Nobbs). Oxford University Press, Oxford.

Bierhoff, H. W. (2002) *Prosocial Behaviour.* Psychology Press, Hove.

Bjornskov, C. (2009) How does social trust affect economic growth? *Economics Working Paper:* 06-2. University of Aarhus, Aarhus School of Business, Department of Economics.

Blumer, H. (1954) What is wrong with social theory? *American Sociological Review* 19(1), 3–10.

Bourdieu, P. (1977) *Outline of a Theory of Practice,* 16th edn. Cambridge University Press, Cambridge.

Bourdieu, P. (1980) Le capital social. *Actes de la Recherche en Sciences Sociales* 31, 2–3.

Bourdieu, P. (1983) The field of cultural production, or: the economic world reversed. *Poetics* 12(4–5), 311–356.

Bourdieu, P. (1986) The forms of capital. In *Handbook of Theory and Research for the Sociology of Education* (ed. J. G. Richardson). Greenwood Publishing Group, Westport, CT, pp. 241–258.

Bowyer, B. T. (2009) The contextual determinants of whites' racial attitudes in England. *British Journal of Political Science* 39(3), 559–586.

Brockerhoff, M. and Eu, H. (1993) Demographic and socioeconomic determinants of female rural to urban migration in Sub-Saharan Africa. *The International Migration Review* 27(3), 557–577.

Brucker, G. (1999) Civic traditions in premodern Italy. *Journal of Interdisciplinary History* 29(3), 357–377.

Burt, R. S. (1992) *The Social Structure of Competition.* Harvard University Press, Cambridge, MA.

Burt, R. S. (2000) The network structure of social capital. *Research in Organizational Behavior* 22, 345–423.

Capo, J., and Halilovich, H. (2013) Localising transnationalism: transborder ties and social realities of the Bosnians and Croats living in two diaspora contexts. *Ethnologie française* 43(2), 291–301.

Caragliu, A., Del Bo, C., de Groot, H. L. F. and Linders, G. J. M. (2012) Cultural determinants of migration. *The Annals of Regional Science* 51(1), 7–32.

Christoforou, A. (2011) Social capital across European countries: individual and aggregate determinants of group membership. *American Journal of Economics and Sociology* 70(3), 699–728.

Christoforou, A. and Davis, J. B. (2014) *Social Capital and Economics: Social Values, Power, and Social Identity,* 20th edn. Routledge, Abingdon.

Cockburn, C., Stakic-Domuz, R. and Hubic, M. (2001) *Women Organizing for Change: A Study of Women's Local Integrative Organizations and the Pursuit of Democracy in Bosnia and Herzegovina.* Medica Zenica u.g., Infoteka, Zeneca.

Coleman, J. S. (1988) Social capital in the creation of human capital. *American Journal of Sociology* 94, S95–S120.

Coleman, J. S. (1993a) *Equality and Achievement in Education.* Westview Press, Boulder, CO.

Coleman, J. S. (1993b) The rational reconstruction of society: 1992 presidential address. *American Sociological Review* 58(1), 1–15.

Collier, P. (1998) *Social Capital and Poverty.* World Bank, Washington, DC.

Collier, P. (2001) Implications of ethnic diversity. *Economic Policy* 16(32), 128–166.

Collier, P. (2002) Social capital and poverty: a microeconomic perspective. In *The Role of Social Capital in Development* (ed. T. Van Bastelaer). Cambridge University Press, Melbourne, pp. 19–41.

Constant, A. F., Gataullina, L. and Zimmermann, K. F. (2009) Ethnosizing immigrants. *Journal of Economic Behavior and Organization* 69(3), 274–287.

Constant, A. F. and Zimmermann, K. F. (2009) Work and money: payoffs by ethnic identity and gender. Institute for the Study of Labor: IZA DP 4275.

Constantinou, S. T. and Diamantides, N. D. (1985) Modeling international migration: determinants of emigration from Greece to the United States, 1820–1980. *Annals of the Association of American Geographers* 75(3), 352–369.

Costa, D. L. and Kahn, E. M. (2003) Understanding the American decline in social capital 1952–1998. *Kyklos* 56(1), 17–46.

Curran, S. R., Garip, F., Chung, C. Y. and Tangchonlatip, K. (2005) Gendered migrant social capital: evidence from Thailand. *Social Forces* 84(1), 225–255.

Curran, S. R. and Rivero-Fuentes, E. (2003) Engendering migrant networks: the case of Mexican migration. *Demography* 40(2), 289–307.

De Andrade, J. H. F., and Delaney, N. B. (2001) Minority return to south-eastern Bosnia and Herzegovina: A Review of the 2000 Return Season. *Journal of Refugee Studies* 14(3), 315–330.

de Haas, H. (2011) The Determinants of Migration Processes and Their Interaction with Migration Policies: An Exploratory Review of the Australian Case. Paper Prepared for the Department of Immigration and Citizenship (DIAC): Australian Government.

Diez, S. G. (2013) Measurement of social capital with the help of time use surveys. *Procedia-Social and Behavioral Sciences* 72, 23–31.

Docquier, F. and Lodigiani, E. (2010) Skilled migration and business networks. *Open Economies Review* 21(4), 565–588.

Docquier, F. and Rapoport, H. (2004) *Skilled Migration: The Perspective of Developing Countries.* World Bank Publications, Washington, DC.

Dunlevy, J. A. (1991) On the settlement patterns of recent Caribbean and Latin immigrants to the United States. *Growth and Change* 22(1), 54–67.

Dyrstad, K. (2012) After ethnic civil war ethno-nationalism in the Western Balkans. *Journal of Peace Research* 49(6), 817–831.

Easterly, W. (2001) The middle class consensus and economic development. *Journal of Economic Growth* 6(4), 317–335.

Easterly, W., Alesina, A. and Baqir, R. (1997) *Public Goods and Ethnic Divisions.* National Bureau of Economic Research, Cambridge, MA.

Easterly, W. and Levine, R. (1997) Africa's growth tragedy: policies and ethnic divisions. *Quarterly Journal of Economics* 112(4), 1203–1250.

Edwards, R., Franklin, J. and Holland, J. (2003) *Families and Social Capital: Exploring the Issues.* London South Bank University, London.

Edwards, R., Franklin, J. and Holland, J. (eds) (2006) *Assessing Social Capital: Concept, Policy and Practice.* Taylor & Francis, London.

Edwards, S. (1999) How effective are capital controls? *The Journal of Economic Perspectives* 13(4), 65–84.

Efendic, A. (2010) *Institutions and Economics Performance in Transition Countries With Special Reference to Bosnia and Herzegovina.* Lambert Academic Publishing, Saarbrücken.

Efendic, A. (2016) Emigration intentions in a post-conflict environment: evidence from Bosnia and Herzegovina. *Post-Communist Economies* 28(3), 335–352.

Efendic, A., Babic, B. and Rebmann, A. (2014a) *Diaspora and Development – Bosnia and Herzegovina.* Embassy of Switzerland in Bosnia and Herzegovina, Sarajevo.

Efendic, A., Silajdzic, S. and Atanasovska, V. (2014b) *Ethnic Tensions and Economic Performance: Bosnia and Herzegovina and Macedonia.* Lambert Academic Publishing, Saarbrücken.

Efendic, A. and Hadziahmetovic, A. (2015) Post-war economic transition in Bosnia and Herzegovina – A Challenging Transformation. In *State-Building and Democratization in Bosnia and Herzegovina,* eds. S. Keil and V. Perry. Ashgate, Farnham, pp. 109–129.

Efendic, A., Mickiewicz, T. and Rebmann, A. (2015) Growth aspirations and social capital: young firms in a post-conflict environment. *International Small Business Journal* 33(5), 537–561.

Efendic, A. and Pugh, G. (2015) Institutional effects on economic performance in post-socialist transition: a dynamic panel analysis. *Acta Oeconomica* 65(4), 503–523.

Efendic, A., Pugh, G. and Adnett, N. (2011) Confidence in formal institutions and reliance on informal institutions in Bosnia and Herzegovina – an empirical investigation using survey data. *Economics of Transition* 19(3), 521–540.

166

Efendic, N. (2010) A view of the Sephardic Romansa in Bosnia-Herzegovina. *Folks Art – Croatian Journal of Ethnology and Folklore Research* 47(2), 163–174.

Eriksen, T. H. (1993) *Ethnicity and Nationalism: Anthropological Perspectives.* Pluto, London.

Escaleras, M. and Register, C. A. (2011) Natural disasters and foreign direct investment. *Land Economics* 87(2), 346–363.

Fearon, J. D. (2003) Ethnic and cultural diversity by country. *Journal of Economic Growth* 8(2), 195–222.

Fehr, E., and Gachter, S. (2000) Fairness and retaliation: the economics of reciprocity. *Journal of Economic Perspectives* 14(3), 159–181.

Fehr, E. and Gachter, S. (2002) Altruistic punishment in humans. *Nature* 415(6868), 137–140.

Field, J. (2003) *Social Capital.* Routledge, New York, NY.

Florida, R. (2002) *The Rise of the Creative Class: And How it's Transforming Work, Leisure, Community and Everyday Life.* Basic Books, New York, NY.

Foley, M. W., and Edwards, B. (1999) Is it time to disinvest in social capital? *Journal of Public Policy* 19(02), 141–173.

Fraser, E. and Lacey, N. (1993) *The Politics of Community.* Harvester/Wheatsheaf, New York, NY.

Fukuyama, F. (1995) *Trust: The Social Virtues and the Creation of Prosperity.* Penguin, London.

Fukuyama, F. (2001) Social capital, civil society and development. *Third World Quarterly* 22(1), 7–20.

Fussell, E. and Massey, D. S. (2004) The limits to cumulative causation: international migration from Mexican Urban Areas. *Demography* 41(1), 151–171.

Garip, F. (2008) Social capital and migration: how do similar resources lead to divergent outcomes? *Demography* 45(3), 591–617.

Gates, S., Hegre, H., Nygård, H. M. and Strand, H. (2012) Development consequences of armed conflict. *World Development* 40(9), 1713–1722.

Gauntlet, D. (2011) *Making is Connecting: The Social Meaning of Creativity.* Polity Press, Cambridge.

Gibson, J., and McKenzie, D. (2011) The microeconomic determinants of emigration and return migration of the best and brightest: evidence from the Pacific. *Journal of Development Economics* 95(1), 18–29.

Giles, M., and Evans, A. (1985) External threat, perceived threat, and group identity. *Social Science Quarterly* 66, 50–66.

Goette, L., Huffman, D. and Meier, S. (2006) *The Impact of Group Membership on Cooperation and Norm Enforcement: Evidence using Random Assignment to Real Social Groups*. Forschungsinstitut zur Zukunft der Arbeit Institute for the Study of Labor. IZA, Discussion Paper: 2020.

Goren, E. (2014) How ethnic diversity affects economic growth. *World Development* 59, 275–297.

Goulbourne, H., and Solomos, J. (2003) Families, ethnicity and social capital. *Social Policy and Society* 2(4), 329–338.

Greve, A., and Salaff, J. W. (2003) Social networks and entrepreneurship. *Entrepreneurship Theory and Practice* 28(1), 1–22.

Grootaert, C., Narayan, D., Jones, V. N. and Woolcock, M. (2004) *Measuring Social Capital: An Integrated Questionnaire*. World Bank Working Paper No. 18. World Bank, Washington, DC.

Grossman, G. M. (2013) Developing social capital through national education: the transformation of teacher education in Turkey. In *Large scale reform and social capital building* (eds. I. M. Saleh, M. S. Khine and I. R. Haslam). Routledge, New York, NY, pp. 127–140.

Hakansson, P., and Sjoholm, F. (2007) Who do you trust? Ethnicity and trust in Bosnia and Herzegovina. *Europe-Asia Studies* 59(6), 961–976.

Halilovich, H. (2012) Trans-local communities in the age of transnationalism: Bosnians in diaspora. *International Migration* 50(1), 162–178.

Halilovich, H. (2013a) Bosnian Austrians: accidental migrants in trans-local and cyber spaces. *Journal of Refugee Studies* 26(4), 524–540.

Halilovich, H. (2013b) *Places of Pain: Forced Displacement, Popular Memory and Trans–local Identities in Bosnian War–torn Communities*. Berghahn Books, Oxford.

Halpern, D. (2005) *Social Capital*. London: Polity.

Haug, S. (2008) Migration networks and migration decision-making. *Journal of Ethnic and Migration Studies* 34(4), 585–605.

Hellermann, C. (2006) Migrating alone: tackling social capital? Women from Eastern Europe in Portugal. *Ethnic and Racial Studies* 29(6), 1135–1152.

Hero, R. E. (2007) *Racial Diversity and Social Capital.* Cambridge University Press, New York.

Hodson, R., Sekulic, D. and Massey, G. (1994) Who were the Yugoslavs? Failed sources of a common identity in the former Yugoslavia. *American Sociological Review* 59(1), 83–97.

Hooghe, M. (2007) Social capital and diversity generalized trust, social cohesion and regimes of diversity. *Canadian Journal of Political Science* 40(3), 709–732.

Horowitz, D. L. (2002) The primordialists. In *Ethnonationalism in the Contemporary World: Walker Connor and the Study of Nationalism* (ed. D. Conversi). Psychology Press, Hove, pp. 72–82.

Jacobs, J. (1961) *The Death and Life of Great American Cities.* Random House, New York, NY.

Jenkins, R. (1992) *The Work of Pierre Bourdieu.* Routledge, London.

Kaasa, A. (2009) Effects of different dimensions of social capital on innovative activity: evidence from Europe at the regional level. *Technovation* 29(3), 218–233.

Kanaiaupuni, S. M. (2000) Reframing the migration question: an analysis of men, women, and gender in Mexico. *Social Forces* 78(4), 1311–1347.

Kaya, A. (2009) *Returnees and Stayers: The Return to a Transformed Society in Bosnia and Herzegovina.* Biligi University, Istanbul.

Kearns, A. and Parkinson, M. (2001) The significance of neighbourhood. *Urban Studies* 38(12), 2103–2110.

Knack, S. (2002) Social capital and the quality of government: evidence from the States. *American Journal of Political Science* 46(4), 772–785.

Knack, S. and Keefer, P. (1997) A Survey of Cross-country Evidence. *Quarterly Journal of Economics*, 112, 1251–1288.

Kwon, S.-W. and Adler, P. S. (2014) Social capital: maturation of a field of research. *Academy of Management Review* 39(4), 412–422.

Kwon, S.-W. and Arenius, P. (2010) Nations of entrepreneurs: a social capital perspective. *Journal of Business Venturing* 25(3), 315–330.

Lake, D. and Rothschild, D. (1998) *The International Spread of Ethnic Conflict: Fear, Diffusion, and Escalation*. Princeton University Press, Princeton, NJ.

Leblang, D. (2010) Familiarity breeds investment: diaspora networks and international investment. *American Political Science Review* 104(3), 584–600.

Lee, E. S. (1966) A theory of migration. *Demography* 3(1), 47–57.

Lemieux, T. (2006) The "Mincer Equation" thirty years after schooling, experience, and earnings. In *Jacob Mincer A Pioneer of Modern Labor Economics* (eds. T. Lemieux and S. Grossbard-Shechtman). Springer, New York, NY, pp. 127–145.

Lesage, J. P. and Ha, C. L. (2012) The impact of migration on social capital: do migrants take their bowling balls with them? *Growth and Change* 43(1), 1–26.

Letki, N. (2008) Does diversity erode social cohesion? Social capital and race in British neighbourhoods. *Political Studies* 56(1), 99–126.

Levitt, P. (1998) Social remittances: migration driven local-level forms of cultural diffusion. *International Migration Review* 32(4), 926–948.

Li, Y., Pickles, A. and Savage, M. (2005) Social capital and social trust in Britain. *European Sociological Review* 21(2), 109–123.

Light, I. (2001) *Social Capital's Unique Accessibility*. Paper presented at the Danish Building and Urban Research/EURA 2001 Conference, Copenhagen.

Lin, N. (1999) Social networks and status attainment. *Annual Review of Sociology* 25, 467–487.

Loury, G. (1977) A dynamic theory of racial income differences. In *Women, Minorities, and Employment Discrimination* (eds P. A. Wallace and A. M. LaMond). Health, Lexington, MA, pp. 86–153.

Marmaros, D. and Sacerdote, B. (2006) How do friendships form? *The Quarterly Journal of Economics* 121(1), 79–119.

Marshall, M. J. and Stolle, D. (2004) Race and the city: neighborhood context and the development of generalized trust. *Political Behavior* 26, 125–153.

Massey, D. S. (1990) Social structure, household strategies, and the cumulative causation of migration. *Population Index* 56(1), 3–26.

Massey, D. S., Arango, J., Hugo, G. *et al.* (1993) Theories of international migration: a review and appraisal. *Population and Development Review* 19, 431–466.

Massey, D. S. and Aysa, M. (2005) Social capital and international migration from Latin America. United Nations Secretariat.

Massey, D. S. and Espinosa, K. E. (1997) What's driving Mexico–US Migration? A theoretical, empirical, and policy analysis. *American Journal of Sociology* 102, 939–999.

Massey, D. S., Goldring, L. and Durand, J. (1994) Continuities in transnational migration: an analysis of nineteen Mexican communities. *American Journal of Sociology* 99, 1492–1533.

McPherson, M., Smith-Lovin, L. and Cook, J. M. (2001) Birds of a feather: homophily in social networks. *Annual Review of Sociology* 27, 415–444.

Miguel, E., Gentler, P. and Levine, D. I. (2005) Does social capital promote industrialisation? Evidence from a rapid industrializer. *The Review of Economics and Statistics* 87(4), 754–762.

Miguel, E., Gertler, P. and Levine, D. I. (2003) *Does Industrialization Build or Destroy Social Networks?* University of California, Berkeley, CA.

Mincer, J. A. (1974) Schooling and earnings. In *Schooling, Experience, and Earnings.* National Bureau of Economic Research, Cambridge, MA, pp. 41–63.

Molyneux, M. (2002) Gender and the silences of social capital: lessons from Latin America. *Development and change* 33(2), 167–188.

Mondéjar-Jiménez, J. A., Gázquez-Abad, J. C. and Gómez-Borja, M. A. (2013) The recreational use value in Spanish protected natural landscapes: proposal for a nature park "Serranía de Cuenca". *International Journal of Environmental Research* 7(2), 337–342.

Montalvo, J. and Reynal-Querol, M. (2005) Ethnicity, political systems and civil wars. *Journal of Conflict Resolution* 46(1), 29–54.

Morrow, V. (1999) Conceptualising social capital in relation to the well-being of children and young people: a critical review. *Sociological Review* 47(4), 744–765.

Myers, S. M. (2000) The impact of religious involvement on migration. *Social Forces* 79(2), 755–783.

Nahapiet, J. and Ghoshal, S. (1998) Social capital, intellectual capital, and the organizational advantage. *Academy of Management Review* 23(2), 242–266.

Nakagawa, Y. and Shaw, R. (2004) Social capital: a missing link to disaster recovery. *International Journal of Mass Emergencies and Disasters* 22(1), 5–34.

Narayan, D. and Cassidy, M. F. (2001) A dimensional approach to measuring social capital: development and validation of a social capital inventory. *Current Sociology* 49(2), 59–102.

Nieminen, T., Koskinen, S., Martelin, T. *et al.* (2008) Measurement and socio-demographic variation of social capital in a large population-based survey. *Social Indicators Research* 85(3), 405–423.

Nooteboom, B. (2007) Social capital, institutions and trust. *Review of Social Economy* 65(1), 29–53.

Nowak, M. A. and Sigmund, K. (2005) Evolution of indirect reciprocity. *Nature* 437(7063), 1291–1298.

Oliver, J. E. (2001) *Democracy in Suburbia.* Princeton University Press, Princeton, NJ.

Onyx, J. and Bullen, P. (2000) Measuring social capital in five communities. *The Journal of Applied Behavioral Science* 36(1), 23–42.

Osborne, E. (2000) Multiculturalism, and ethnic conflict: a rent-seeking perspective. *Kyklos* 53(4), 509–526.

Ostrom, E. (1999) Social capital: a fading or a fundamental concept. In *Social Capital: A Multifaceted Perspective* (eds P. Dasgupta and I. Serageldin). World Bank, Washington, DC, pp. 172–214.

Ottaviano, G. I. and Peri, G. (2006) The economic value of cultural diversity: evidence from US cities. *Journal of Economic Geography* 6(1), 9–44.

Palloni, A., Massey, D. S., Ceballos, M. *et al.* (2001) Social capital and international migration: a test using information on family networks. *American Journal of Sociology* 106(5), 1262–1298.

Patsiurko, N., Campbell, J. L. and Hall, J. A. (2012) Measuring cultural diversity: ethnic, linguistic and religious fractionalization in the OECD. *Ethnic and Racial Studies* 35(2), 195–217.

Pieterse, J. N. (2003) Social capital and migration: beyond ethnic economies. *Ethnicities* 3(1), 29–58.

Petrovic, J. (2007) *Ničiji ljudi.* Beograd: Socijalna misao, 2007.

Polletta, F. and Jasper, J. M. (2011) Collective identity and social movements. *Annual Review of Sociology* 27(1), 283–305.

Popova, Z. (2009) The Role of Social Capital for Post-Ethnic-Conflict Reconstruction. PhD thesis, University of Bath, Bath.

Porobic, S. and Mameledzija, S. (2013) *They are Doing it for Themselves! Partner up with Competent Returnees and CSOs in Returnee Communities if you Aim to Achieve the Sustainability of Return in BiH.* Policy Development Fellowships Program 2013–2014. Open Society Foundation, New York, NY.

Portes, A. (1998) Social capital: its origins and applications in modern sociology. *Annual Review of Sociology* 24, 1–24.

Portes, A. (2000) The two meanings of social capital. *Sociological Forum* 15(1), 1–12.

Posner, D. (2000) *Ethnic Fractionalization in Africa: How Should it be Measured? What Does it Explain About Economic Growth?* World Bank Development Research Group Seminar, Vol. 29. World Bank, Washington, DC.

Povrzanovic-Frykman, M. (2002) Violence and the re-discovery of place. *Ethnologia Europaea* 32(2), 69–88.

Putnam, R. D. (1993) The prosperous community. *The American Prospect* 4(13), 35–42.

Putnam, R. D. (1995) Bowling alone: America's declining social capital. *Journal of Democracy* 6(1), 65–78.

Putnam, R. D. (2000) Bowling alone: America's declining social capital. In *Culture and Politics* (eds L. Crothers and C. Lockhart). Palgrave Macmillan, New York, NY, pp. 223–234.

Putnam, R. D. (2001) *Bowling Alone: The Collapse and Revival of American Community.* Simon & Schuster, New York, NY.

Putnam, R. D. (2007) E Pluribus unum: civic engagement in a diverse and changing society. *Scandinavian Political Studies* 30(2), 137–174.

Quibria, M. G. (2003) *The Puzzle of Social Capital A Critical Review.* ERD Working Paper No. 40. Manilia: Asian Development Bank.

Ravenstein, E. G. (1889) The laws of migration. *Journal of the Statistical Society of London* 52(2), 241–305.

Rebmann, A., Efendic, A. and Mickiewicz, T. (2017) Nascent enterprises and growth aspirations in a post-conflict environment: the role of social capital. In *Routledge Handbook of Entrepreneurship in Developing*

Economies (eds C. Williams and A. Gurtoo). Routledge, New York, NY, pp. 70–89.

Righi, A. (2013) Measuring social capital: official statistics initiatives in Italy. *Procedia-Social and Behavioral Sciences* 72, 4–22.

Rose, R. (1999) *Making Openness Work.* John Hopkins University Press, Baltimore, MD.

Ross, L. M. (1982) Testing control theory and differential association: a causal modeling approach. *American Sociological Review* 47, 489–504.

Rothschild, J. (1981) *Ethnopolitics, A Conceptual Framework.* Columbia University Press, New York, NY.

Rothstein, B., and Stolle, D. (2008) The state and social capital: an institutional theory of generalized trust. *Comparative Politics* 40(4), 441–459.

Ruttan, L. M. (2006) Sociocultural heterogeneity and the commons. *Current Anthropology* 47(5), 843–853.

Savioli, M. and Patuelli, R. (2016) *Social Capital, Institutions and Policymaking.* Kiel Institute for the World Economy, Economics Discussion Papers 2016–26.

Semenas, V. (2014) Ethnic diversity and social capital at the community level: effects and implications for policymakers. *Inquiries Journal* 6(4), 1–2.

Shucksmith, M. (2000) Endogenous development, social capital and social inclusion: perspectives from LEADER in the UK. *Sociologia Ruralis* 40(2), 208–218.

Smith, S. S. and Kulynych, J. (2002) It may be social, but why is it capital? The social construction of social capital and the politics of language. *Politics and Society* 30(1), 149–186.

Sobel, J. (2002) Can we trust social capital? *Journal of Economic Literature* 40(1), 139–154.

Sonderskov, K. M. (2011) Does generalized social trust lead to associational membership? Unravelling a bowl of well-tossed spaghetti. *European Sociological Review* 27(4), 419–434.

Stamm, S. (2006) Social networks among return migrants to post-war Lebanon. ETH Zurich and CIS Working Paper. University of Zurich, Zurich.

Stark, O. (1991) *The Migration of Labor.* Cambridge: Blackwell.

174

Stark, O. (2004) On the Economics of Refugee Flows. Review of Development Economics, *Wiley Blackwell*, 8(2), 325–329.

Stark, O. and Bloom, D. E. (1985) The new economics of labor migration. *The American Economic Review* 75(2),173–178.

Stark, O., Helmenstein, C. and Prskawetz, A. (1997) A brain gain with a brain drain. *Economics Letters* 55(2), 227–234.

Stefansson, A. (2004) Sarajevo suffering: homecoming and the hierarchy of homeland hardship. In *Homecomings: Unsettling Paths of Return* (eds F. Markowitz and A. Stefansson). Lexington, Lanham, MD, pp. 54–75.

Stephan, U., Uhlaner, K. M. and Stride, C. (2015) Institutions and social entrepreneurship: the role of institutional coids, institutional support, and institutional configurations. *Journal of International Business Studies* 46(3), 308–331.

Stolle, D. and Hooghe, M. (2005) Inaccurate, exceptional, one-sided or irrelevant? The debate about the alleged decline of social capital and civic engagement in Western societies. *British Journal of Political Science* 35(1), 149–167.

Stone, W. and Hughes, J. (2002) Measuring Social Capital: Toward a Standardised Approach. Paper presented at the 2002 Australasian Evaluation Society International Conference October/November 2002 – Wollongong Australia.

Stryker, S. and Burke, P. J. (2000) The past, present, and future of an identity theory. *Social Psychology Quarterly* 63(4), 284–297.

Taylor, E. J. (1999) The new economics of labour migration and the role of remittances in the migration process. *International Migration* 37(1), 63–88.

Tonkiss, F. (2000) Trust, social capital and economy. In *Trust and Civil Society* (eds. F. Tonkiss, A. Passey, N. Fenton, and L. Hems). Macmillan, Basingstoke, pp. 72–89.

Tzanakis, M. (2013) Social capital in Bourdieu's, Coleman's and Putnam's theory: empirical evidence and emergent measurement issues. *Educate* 13(2), 2–23.

UNDP (2007) *The Silent Majority Speaks.* UNDP in BiH, Sarajevo.

UNDP (2009) *The Ties That Bind – Social Capital in Bosnia and Herzegovina. National Human Development Report 2009.* UNDP BiH, Sarajevo.

Uphoff, N. (2000) Understanding social capital: learning from the analysis and experience of participation. In *Social Capital: A Multifaceted Perspective* (eds P. Dasgupta and I. Serageldin). World Bank Publications, Washington, DC, pp. 215–249.

Uslaner, E. M. (2002) *The Moral Foundations of Trust*. Cambridge University Press, New York, NY.

Valenta, M. and Ramet, S. P. (eds) (2011) *The Bosnian Diaspora: Integration in Transnational Communities*. Ashgate, Farnham.

van der Gaag, M. and Snijders, T. A. (2005) The resource generator: social capital quantification with concrete items. *Social Networks* 27(1), 1–29.

Vanhoutte, B. and Hooghe, M. (2012) Do diverse geographical contexts lead to diverse friendship networks? A multilevel analysis of Belgian survey data. *International Journal of Intercultural Relations* 36(3), 343–352.

Waring, T. M. (2011) Ethnic forces in collective action: diversity, dominance, and irrigation in Tamil Nadu. *Ecology and Society* 16(4), 1.

Westlund, H. and Adam, F. (2010) Social capital and economic performance: A meta-analysis of 65 studies. *European Planning Studies* 18(6), 893–919.

Whitt, S. (2010) Institutions and ethnic trust: evidence from Bosnia. *Europe-Asia Studies* 62(2), 271–292.

Woolcock, M. (1998) Social capital and economic development: toward a theoretical synthesis and policy framework. *Theory and Society* 27(2), 151–208.

Worpole, K. and Knox, K. (2007) *The Social Value of Public Spaces*. Joseph Rowntree Foundation, York.

Zbinden, M., Dahinden, J. and Efendic, A. (2016) Rethinking the debate about the diversity of migration in South-East Europe. In Diversity of Migration in South-East Europe (eds. M. Zbinden, J. Dahinden and A. Efendic). Bern, Peter Lang, pp. 7–34.

Notes about the Authors

Adnan Efendic is an associate professor of economics at the School of Economics and Business, University of Sarajevo. He is an affiliate fellow at CERGE-EI, Prague and CISAR, Sarajevo. He is an applied economist and his research has been based on different methodologies, including, in particular, metaregression analysis, dynamic panel analysis and structural equation modelling. He is an institutional economist and his current research interest is focused on the link between formal and informal institutions in the Western Balkan region.

Bojana Babic currently works as an independent researcher while proceeding with her PhD studies. She holds two MA degrees in international businesses and migration studies from universities in Italy, Germany and Norway. Her research has been developed around different issues in migration field, including cities, space, development, health and gender. Some of her papers have already been published in leading journals.

Anna Rebmann is lecturer in economics and international business at the Economics and Strategy Group, Aston Business School, Aston University. Her research focuses on institutions, social capital and entrepreneurship.

Index

INTERDISCIPLINARY STUDIES ON CENTRAL AND EASTERN EUROPE

Edited by
Christian Giordano, Nicolas Hayoz & Jens Herlth

This series focuses on the political, economic and cultural changes in Eastern Europe and the former Soviet Union. It offers a platform for inter-disciplinary research on this multifaceted part of the world. The focus lies mainly on current and recent developments in societies and political systems; but research on cultural and historical backgrounds has its place here, too. The range of disciplines includes political science, history, and social anthropology, but also philosophy, cultural studies, and literary criticism. The articles are written in English.

Band 20   Adnan Efendic, Bojana Babic & Anna Rebmann
           Social Capital, Migration, Ethnic Diversity and Economic
           Performance.
           Multidisciplinary Evidence from South-East Europe.
           183 pp. 2017.
           ISBN 978-3-0343-2772-5